ADVANCE PRAISE FOR

Defiance in Exile:
Syrian Refugee Women in Jordan

"*Defiance in Exile* is a powerful testimony of hope despite war, unimaginable heartbreak, and economic hardship. It is a book that delivers on its promise to truly reveal what it is like to be in a refugee camp. And it closes with a profoundly moving message of the need to care for and be in solidarity with the oppressed."

—Dawn Chatty, author of *Syria: The Making and Unmaking of a Refuge State*

"This hortatory collection of Syrian women refugees' stories, this *j'accuse* against the evil Asad regime and a willfully oblivious world, is a call to awareness and action. Can you read these stories of loss, madness, despair, claustrophobia, and resilience without screaming that something must be done?"

—Miriam Cooke, author of *Dancing in Damascus*

"If there is a 'must read' book inspired by what has happened to Syria and Syrians over the past decade, this is it. In telling the gripping stories of Syrian refugee women dealing with dispossession while leading their families and affirming themselves, *Defiance in Exile* speaks with penetrating insight and jarring directness to each one of us. No one will come away from reading this book unmoved or unchanged."

—Ambassador Frederic C. Hof, diplomat-in-residence at Bard College and former US special envoy to Syria

"If you want to be aware of the desperate life of Syrian refugees living in camps outside their lost home country, this book is a must. *Defiance in Exile* reflects an urgent call to do something about the Syrian refugee crisis."

—Nikolaos van Dam, former ambassador of the Netherlands and special envoy for Syria and author of *Destroying a Nation*

"The stories found within *Defiance in Exile* are an altogether human story of our species' ability to enact unimaginable harm and suffering, while simultaneously illuminating the human capacity for hope and empathy. Athamneh and Masud are masterful storytellers, and they narrate the lives of the individuals they encounter with an emotional richness that brings the reader into the experiences without any hint of voyeurism."

—Hillary J. Haldane, co-editor of
Applying Anthropology to Gender-Based Violence

"*Defiance in Exile* provides compelling first-person testimony of Syrian women's experiences in the al-Zaatari refugee camp in Jordan. The accounts are vivid and well-presented, and we need to hear such voices to counteract the often hostile rhetoric about Syrian refugees that one hears in North Atlantic countries."

—Kim Shively, author of *Islam in Modern Turkey*

DEFIANCE
IN EXILE

DEFIANCE
IN EXILE

Syrian Refugee Women in Jordan

WAED ATHAMNEH

with Muhammad Masud

University of Notre Dame Press

Notre Dame, Indiana

Library of Congress Control Number: 2021943083

ISBN: 978-0-268-20116-6 (hardback)
ISBN: 978-0-268-20117-3 (paperback)
ISBN: 978-0-268-20115-9 (WebPDF)
ISBN: 978-0-268-20118-0 (Epub)

Ghassan,

The idea of this book came to your mother before you were born. The visits to al-Zaatari camp took place shortly after you were born. Your mother and father worked on this manuscript while you provided them with all the love and patience a child possesses, making our mission an enjoyable one. This book will eventually see the light, reaching the hands of those who seek knowledge and knock on its wide-open doors. It is our hope that you will grow up to be the man you want to be, never forgetting your duty to your fellow humans, wherever they may be.

CONTENTS

FOREWORD

Currently three of four political refugees in the world are Muslim. Compounded by environmental refugees, warns the writer Ziauddin Sardar, this ratio could change to four of five by 2035.[1] The "middle belt" area of the world, from Morocco in the west to Indonesia in the east, is a zone of Muslim majorities. In addition, it is a zone vulnerable to both political and environmental precarity. Only a massive exercise of human will directed toward stemming political instability and effecting a change in human behavior in order to redress climate change can avert the dire forecast of catastrophes for this middle belt region and many other regions around the world. Needless to say, significant populations of Christians, Hindus, Buddhists, Druze, Alawites, and other faith traditions, as well as people without faith traditions, are also located in this middle belt. Nature in its brutality does not discriminate and inflicts its rigors on friend and foe. But nature also rewards human behavior if the stewardship of the environment occurs in a timely manner. In conditions of precarity, as experiences from Rwanda to Bosnia show, the best of neighbors brutally turn on each other. Faith, class, and ethnicity often serve merely as a fig leaf to justify the worst in human conduct. We are bound by faith, common sense, and a concern for human dignity to avert these disasters at any cost. Hence, this task requires human solidarity and care as a minimum.

In *Defiance in Exile*, Waed Athamneh and Muhammad Masud offer us many moving portraits of the perilous situation of Syrian refugees in camps in Jordan. Simultaneously, we are inspired by the heroic acts and resilience of refugees clasping onto faith and dignity.

This book rightly focuses on the plight of women and their families. Why so many women feel compelled to leave hearth and home to become refugees is surely obvious. Women fear not only for themselves; often women's most overwhelming concern is to protect their offspring from the dangers of certain death, especially if they are forced to fend for themselves in situations of war. Escaping death is one thing. To escape a life of debilitating poverty is another, despite the best charitable support available from time to time.

Wherever refugees go they have to begin a life of normality anew. But for every refugee, normal is never the same. It is always a "new normal," one that is frequently shadowed by pain, grief, and loss. Yet sometimes there are flickers of hope, what the authors describe as a glimmer of light. Athamneh and Masud have given us one detailed portrait of the lives of Syrian refugees who were driven out of Syria by a pitiless civil war.

The Arab Spring of December 2011, which triggered peaceful protests for democracy in Syria and then quickly degenerated into violence, is now a distant memory. Momentarily, the Arab Spring brought hope to many for a better and humane future. In most places where the spark of political hope briefly shone, apart from Tunisia, the forces of political totalitarianism and immoral geopolitical machinations undermined the democratic ideals fostered by millions of people in the middle belt. Capricious alliances with the Syrian people by their neighbors brought them to the precipice of a country emptied of its people. Roughly 5.5 million Syrians live as refugees around the world, and some 6.1 million are internally displaced people.

Surely, the world should never forget the plight of the Jewish people as refugees over time but especially their devastating fate in modern Europe. Yet for the hundreds of thousands of Palestinian people who were violently displaced from their homeland by the establishment of the state of Israel, it was up to artists and writers to share the experiences of these refugees whose aspirations were repeatedly shattered. The Palestinian struggle serves as a sobering reminder to Syrians and all other refugees around the world of the challenges that lie ahead.

The plight of refugees in the middle belt can be gleaned from the writings of the late Palestinian poet Mahmoud Darwish, whose oeuvre is marked by the endless status of Palestinians in exile and of homelessness. In his extended prose-poetry reflection, *Memory for Forgetfulness*, on the 1982 Israeli invasion of Lebanon and the ensuing Lebanese civil war, he evocatively describes how the express purpose of the war was to dislodge Palestinians who had taken refuge in the surrounding areas of Beirut for decades. In compelling and imaginative prose, Darwish captures their predicament in the ordinary and everyday struggles for survival. Nothing can excel how Darwish mixes displacement, violence, and the hope of the everyday as fostered by refugees; he does not allow us to forget that he, too, was a refugee.

Describing the plight of Palestinian refugees during the Israeli bombing of Beirut in 1982, Darwish writes, "They came in search of a place to sleep, on a square meter open to wind and patriotic songs. But what the primitive daggers forgot to do is being done by fighter planes, which haven't stopped shelling this human continuity. Where's all this leading? Where? From massacre to slaughter have my people been led, and still they bring forth offspring in debris-filled stopping places, flash victory signs, and prepare wedding feasts. Does a bomb have grandchildren? Us. Does a piece of shrapnel have grandparents? Us."[2]

Imagine refugees and their offspring becoming more desperate in a bid to seek refuge elsewhere by escaping their first place of safety. Describing refugees twice over as the grandchildren of bombs and the grandparents of shrapnel—an ironic and brutal twist of language—remains true to the painful and mournful reality. Darwish scripts the violence unleashed on Palestinian bodies as a genealogy of endless violence where bombs and shrapnel produce real descendants, like grandparents and grandchildren, a metaphor that takes your breath away.

Whenever refugees try to re-create normality, by hanging a painting on a wall, for example, almost instantaneously violence shatters it. In Darwish's words, "But no sooner did we hang a painting than a car bomb exploded, destroying all the arrangements. And no sooner did I rest my head on my left elbow, waiting for my coffee, than I found myself outside."³ What a minute ago was a coffeehouse now stands transformed into an open-air space, with walls shattered by the blast and the poet as a witness, counting his blessings to have survived this one.

For those of us who care about the human condition and the oppressed—those who live in stable democracies or in fragile states—the message of care and solidarity for the oppressed cannot be ignored. The outcasts and the downtrodden in the idiom of the Muslim scripture, the Qur'ān, are known as the *mustaḍ ʿafūn*, literally, "those who have been rendered weak by dint of circumstances and material conditions." Those of us who have the resources are tasked with the imperative to meet our moral duty to those who are oppressed in the world. The invitation to act cannot be clearer.

> Why would you not fight
> In the cause of God,
> and oppressed men, women, and children
> who say, "Our Lord, get us out of this town,
> whose people are oppressors.
> And provide us a protector from You,
> and provide us a helper from You." (Qur'ān 4:75)⁴

Throughout this book Athamneh and Masud remind us of this summons from God and the promptings of common human decency, often repeated in different ways in scriptures or secular documents of humanity. "Cursed be anyone who deprives the alien, the orphan, and the widow of justice," says the Bible.⁵ In the service of this sacred duty the Christian teaching invites all people to say, "Amen." In other words, we affirm our readiness to shoulder our responsibility, which is what fighting in the cause of God means: to intervene and make things better. In many ways fighting for the "other" is also the struggle to assert and reinforce one's own humanity. The authors of this book write insightfully when they say, "To protect your children is to protect yourself. To fight for their rights and freedoms is to fight for your own. To pursue a better future for them is to push yourself to find and understand your weaknesses and fears and to choose to listen to your inner self, to refuse to submit to a life that offers less."

As humans caught up in the struggles of life, whether as survivors or thrivers, we require constant reminders of the general conditions of the world that ought to be within our moral horizon. "The struggle of man against power," the novelist Milan Kundera said a while ago, "is the struggle of memory against forgetting."[6] By bringing us stories from the inhabitants of al-Zaatari Camp, the authors have fulfilled a major responsibility to make us aware of a reality often forgotten. Yet the issue of refugees is the most important human rights and humanitarian question of our times. I trust that this book will serve to awaken within us the call to conscience and give new impetus to our constructive and critical role in world affairs as citizens of the world and in human fellowship.

Ebrahim Moosa
Mirza Family Professor of Islamic Thought and Muslim Society
Keough School of Global Affairs, University of Notre Dame
September 29, 2020

Notes

1. Ziauddin Sardar, "Introduction: Postnormal Horizons," in *Critical Muslim*, special issue, *Futures*, ed. Ziauddin Sardar, 29 (January–March 2019): 13.

2. Mahmoud Darwish, *Memory for Forgetfulness: August, Beirut, 1982* (Berkeley: University of California Press, 2013), 90.

3. Ibid., 71.

4. Thomas Cleary, *The Qur'an: A New Translation* (n.p.: Starlatch Press, 2004), 42.

5. Deuteronomy 27:19. Wayne A. Meeks et al., *The HarperCollins Study Bible: New Revised Standard Version*, fully rev. std. ed. (San Francisco: HarperSanFrancisco, 1993), 309–10.

6. Milan Kundera, *The Book of Laughter and Forgetting* (New York: Penguin Books, 1981), 4.

A Mission Is Born

The three brothers were nine, eleven, and thirteen. The boys worked nonstop, polishing a large pickup truck. Meanwhile, a man watched from the corner of the auto body shop. The smell of his cigarettes and the loud, grunting sound he made while sipping his cheap coffee were constant reminders that he was still there.

An intense odor of strong chemicals filled the dark room.

The nine-year-old used a kitchen sponge to scrub the inside of the truck. The small sponge was falling apart as he soaked it in a chemical concoction that could clean anything, or at least that's what the shop advertised. The eleven-year-old and the thirteen-year-old handled the outside of the truck, applying polish and paint with their fingers. They used dirty rags and loads of solvents and fluids on every part of the truck to give it that brand-new look.

The children worked in silence. They worked without speaking to each other. They handled the hazardous products with their bare hands. They worked with no gloves or masks, no protective gear of any kind. They just *worked*.

An old radio played in the background, interrupted only by a commanding voice that came from the corner of the shop. The man gave the children instructions from time to time. He was the proprietor of the shop, and they were his workers. He rarely spoke, but when he did, the children listened. They also obeyed. They obeyed without delay, without question, without uttering a word. They obeyed without eye contact.

The three boys were Syrian refugees.

The shop was on the outskirts of Irbid, Jordan's third-largest city, a mere twelve miles from the Syrian border. It is also where we grew up and spent most of our young lives. After spending years abroad, we were just beginning to realize the effects of the Syrian refugee crisis in the city.

The scorching July sun, blended with the smoke and smell of burning gasoline from half-century-old cars, made this rough and industrial part of the city particularly unbearable. This was no place for children.

We inched closer to the owner, trying to get a sense of why this was happening. He finally pulled out some rusty old chairs and offered us a seat.

"It seems he knows what he is doing," we said, pointing to the older brother, who was applying black polish to the body of the car with his bare hands.

"Yes. This is American polish. It's the best in the market. Top quality," the owner answered and took a loud sip of his coffee.

"But this boy. He seems focused. What's his story?" we asked.

"He is *maskeen* [simple], you know. I gave them a job. I did it for God. I am just trying to help them. Their father died in Syria. Their mother is sick. They have nobody here to look after them."

The three boys earned a total of US$15 a day: $5 each for a day's work. The availability of such cheap, expendable labor made it possible for businesses to take advantage of the situation. Some employers also exploited the initial lack of regulations dealing with Syrian refugee workers. The country's lawmakers had struggled to deal with the influx of refugees in the country.

As time passed, the government allowed some Syrians to obtain work permits and introduced a regulated leave system for refugees living in camps. However, new regulations could not fix Jordan's already frail economy, which could not create enough jobs for citizens and refugees.

Cities such as Irbid witnessed a major change in the wake of the Syrian crisis. Urban centers became key hosts for refugee communities. Many refugees arrived in search of employment, hoping to find a job—*any* job—in major cities during such difficult times. But when there were not enough jobs, Syrian refugees often had to take difficult and hazardous jobs at low wages. Low as it may be, if you did the work, you got the pay, right?

Well, sometimes you did.

Syrian refugees occupied a gray area in Jordan. Many were not legally permitted to work. This left them at the mercy of employers. When Syrian refugees went unpaid, they could not report it to the authorities. Often, employers simply terminated workers and brought in new ones without consequences. Lawmakers and decision makers in Jordan have recently given much-needed attention to the labor conditions of Syrian refugees in the country, which has resulted in institutionalizing new regulations allowing Syrian refugees to work, providing they adhere to these regulations.

The constant threat of being deported made things worse. As we came to learn later in al-Zaatari Camp, there was a specific expression used there to describe this threat: "We'll hurl you" back to Syria. The word literally means "to swing or launch," as one would a shell or a missile.

When we talked to the eldest of the brothers, he was understandably reluctant to give any information. Why should he trust anyone? Adults were carrying on this atrocious war and causing children like himself to suffer. Even then, as he worked in that awful body shop, an adult was exploiting his hard labor.

But, that young boy emphatically told us, "*Al-hamdullilah* [Thank you, God], at least we're not in the camp."

It was not the first time we had heard this. We had been speaking to refugee families in the city of Irbid and surrounding villages. The one sentence echoed so many times was, "We are thankful we are not in the camp." When we asked what that meant, we often heard, "You have to go there and see for yourselves."

Umm Omar had told us so. Umm Omar was a seventy-nine-year-old Syrian woman who had seen it all. She had lived under the Assad regime's tyranny since the 1970s. At her old age, Umm Omar had made a difficult journey to seek refuge in Jordan.

Umm Omar was also our neighbor in Irbid. She came out to her apartment's balcony early in the day and sat there, observing the busy streets. Things that sometimes bothered us did not seem to even cross her mind. The screaming kids who played soccer until 2 a.m.? Well, they were just fine.

We greeted Umm Omar every morning and secretly waited for her well-wishes and prayer of *tawfeeq* (good luck). She had the warmth and kindness of a grandmother, one who had seen it all but was still smiling. That was powerful to us: whatever Assad took away, he failed to take that.

We asked Umm Omar about al-Zaatari. She had few words to say, but for us, these words were enough: "The injustice we saw in our lifetime cannot be described. We could not think of who we are or what we wanted. Thoughts scared us, but not anymore. We paid the price, and there is no going back. God help the women in this war. They have to act strong and listen to everyone else's concerns, but who listens to them? It's a long story that you have to hear from those who own it."

That day, we made Umm Omar a promise. We would find these women and listen to their stories, and then we would tell them to the world.

At that moment, our mission was born.

What's it like to be a refugee in a camp? we wondered. We were about to see for ourselves.

Over the following months, we would visit al-Zaatari and hear Syrian refugee women tell their stories. As some made the choice to speak out, others chose not to.

A Story of Many

One of the ways the word *story* is used in Arabic is to ask about distress. Indeed, stories coming out of Syria revealed Assad's cruelty long before the Syrian uprising started. Many were known by Syrians and their neighbors in countries such as Lebanon and Jordan.

Of the many stories from Syria we had heard, one in particular struck a chord with us. It was about a young woman jailed in Assad's prisons. The Syrian writer Michel Kilo, who was imprisoned at the time for criticizing Assad, revealed the story.

Over the years, Michel had developed a simple relationship with one of the prison guards. At one point, the guard even secretly gave Michel a nail clipper and told him to use it with caution. If he was caught helping, the guard warned, he would be sent to Tadmor for three years. Tadmor Prison was located in the Syrian desert and had a reputation for being one of the regime's harshest.

One night, the guard entered Michel's cell at three o'clock in the morning. He took Michel in secret to another cell and stopped at the door. The guard then made a strange request.

"There is a child inside this cell. I want you to tell him a story."

"A . . . story? What kind of story?"

"Any story. Aren't you educated? Just tell the child a story."

Once the door cracked open, Michel noticed a terrorized young woman sitting in the fetal position in a dark corner. Next to her stood a five-year-old boy. In shock, Michel attempted to assure the frightened young woman he meant no harm—that he was there because he was ordered to tell a story.

Michel approached the child and started telling a simple story. "There was once a bird . . . "

What the child said next left Michel in shock: "What's a bird?"

Michel tried to explain, "It sat on a tree . . . "

"What's a tree?" the child asked.

Horrified, Michel began to realize that the child had no idea what these words meant. The reason? He had never seen any of these things. The child was born inside the cell and had never seen the outside world. The young woman was imprisoned as a hostage because her father, who was wanted by the regime, escaped to Amman. She had been systemically raped for years and delivered this poor child, who knows nothing in life but the walls of his prison cell.

But were stories like this reaching the world? Not really.

In the United States, people who seek to learn about the Syrian crisis have only a small number of sources. Some learn about it from viral images and videos about the conflict, such as those of Omran Daqneesh and Alan Kurdi. Omran sat in horror in an ambulance after a regime airstrike in Aleppo. Alan was not so lucky. His family tried to reach Europe via the Mediterranean after they paid smugglers thousands of dollars. They boarded an overloaded inflatable boat with no life vests. Alan was only three when the boat sank. Alan drowned, along with his mother and brother.

Other people rely on political conversation to learn about the Syrian crisis. But there is no conversation; the issue of Syrian refugees is divisive. It is hard to find a coherent reality in the midst of all the noise. More than ever before, ideological positions determine political reactions. Others seek to learn from the media, but it too is divided across party lines and political interests.

There is little knowledge about the Syrian crisis, even at the highest level of politics. When the Libertarian candidate Gary Johnson was asked what he would do about what was happening in Aleppo, he famously responded, "What is Aleppo?" If even presidential candidates have no clue about the issue, why would regular people?

The truth of the matter is that those who actively seek to learn about Syrian refugees will find it challenging. Meanwhile, the Syrian conflict has been getting worse. The continued violence has forced Syrians to seek shelter around the world, causing a global refugee crisis.

By 2017, the Syrian refugee population had exceeded five million outside Syria. Men, women, and children take treacherous journeys that endanger their lives, walking in extreme weather and risking their lives and that of their children to reach refuge. Many lose their lives on these journeys. Those who make it live amid growing anti-refugee sentiment. Many live in fear of being blamed as a group for the actions of a single refugee.

In the United States, an atmosphere of fear and mistrust has skewed the perception of Syrian refugees. One of its clearest results is a ban on the entry of refugees from Syria and other Muslim-majority countries. One of the reasons for this is the spreading of myths about Syrian refugees. Some myths claim refugees are young men trying to infiltrate the United States. Others claim that refugees have no plans to return home.

Syrian women are targeted with specific myths that cast them as voiceless, oppressed, and silent victims. As they listen to these myths about them in the media, they are rarely given equal voice to participate in the conversation about themselves.

Of course, these myths are far from the reality. Politicians have used the issue of refugees to incite mistrust and further their own agendas. But it is not just the politicians: the real problem is that we do not get to hear stories from refugees themselves but instead hear them from those watching their struggle from far away.

This is precisely why this book came to fruition. We wanted to engage with Syrian refugee women through their own voices. Instead of *talking about* refugees, these narratives allow us to *listen to* refugees as they tell their stories. Only then can we emerge with a better understanding of the global refugee crisis. And only then will we start to see their plight.

It might be the world's largest Syrian refugee camp, but that is not why we went to al-Zaatari. We went because it gave us the chance to listen to Syrian refugee women. Of the many things we learned, one was clearest: refugee women are not voiceless. In fact, they have a lot to say. They are determined to share stories worth telling.

The Missing Voice

Imagine that you are asked to write a book about your life. Your story must recount every hurdle, pleasure, pain, or fear you have ever experienced. The book would be a reflection of your whole character, your whole life. It would be all that people would ever know about you. Anything you leave out will be as though it never happened, no matter how important it is to you. You have 150 pages.

Could you do it? Suddenly, a book seems small. How can you fit in everything? You dealt with so much. You overcame this challenge when you were that age, conquered that hurdle but struggled with this one, felt accepted here but not there. You had to do this, face that. So many things to say—everything you ever were or will be.

The same is true for refugees. If a whole book is not enough to represent a single human experience, how could one story do so in only a few pages? The voices of refugee women are powerful and compelling—sometimes haunting. Each story, however, remains just a snippet of a refugee woman's experience. It is not a representation of her whole life, which cannot be reduced to a single story. The better way to learn about refugees is to take the stories they have shared as a way to *expand* but not define their experiences—a way to resist preconceived ideas about their lives.

Some refugees show disillusionment with the world and the existence of any real justice in it, at least for them. One refugee we met at the camp described how she was constantly approached by Western journalists asking for happy stories. They all asked similar questions. At first, she answered thoroughly, but after a while the interviews became meaningless. She felt the journalists had already decided what they wanted to hear before even talking to her. What they wanted was not what she had to say but a story of success and triumph amid the disaster.

Others show fierce determination in the face of the conflict. Suad is an example of defiance in the face of Assad's brutality. Suad refuses to give away her free will, which very few of us do. She admits that she is not perfect; she has flaws like everyone else, but she works hard to improve her life and that of others. She inspires fellow refugee women. Suad's strength and determination stems not from her perfection but from her fragility and imperfection. She accepts fear, challenges, faults, anything. "Assad can use whatever weapons and techniques to humiliate and coerce us. Submission is not on the table," Syrian women refugees collectively remarked.

Tibah is another striking example of the limitless force of life. She believes in her ability and potential, and she refuses to surrender to circumstances. She is undeterred by the lack of opportunity for women in the camp. She relentlessly seeks work and takes on new responsibilities. Tibah is many women in one: she is the breadwinner of her family, the mother of her children, the wife of her husband, the friend and supporter of her sister-in-law. She, too, is the strong voice of refugee women.

It is worth noting that as we reviewed the interview material, we recognized the limitations imposed on us by the structure of the camp. We were not allowed to wander freely or visit random caravans, as we had planned. Camp officials told us that they were offering us their necessary assistance to avoid "dangerous" districts and stay in districts that were "safe." They selected and guided us to the caravans of certain women. This means that while we ideally wanted to meet a random selection of women from different districts in the camp, we did not choose the caravans we visited or the women we interviewed; rather, they were selected for us. In addition, two women came to the caravan where Waed was conducting an interview and asked to be included, saying, "We heard there is a researcher here, so we came to talk to you." We did not see or hear anything to suggest that our guides had been directed to introduce us to specific people in order to pursue a particular agenda or that the women we interviewed had been encouraged to tell particular stories. However, camp employees get to know many of the inhabitants, and it is possible that they may have connected us with particular women in an attempt to highlight particular narratives.

Syrian women offer glimpses of their lives in the stories presented here. They struggle with a reality that is far from ideal and speak of their plight as refugees, but they also speak of an enduring spirit that often defies and resists that harsh reality. This book registers an aspect of Syrian women's defiance in the face of tyranny and their resolve to create a new life for their children in a country that is not their own.

The publication of this book marks the first phase in fulfilling a promise made in early 2015 in the middle of the Mafraq desert in Jordan to remarkable Syrian women. The promise of sharing their stories with the world does not count as fulfilled unless you do your part as a fellow human being. You see, first, these women are human beings, like the rest of us. Second, they are grandmothers, mothers, wives, daughters, sisters, and so on. And third, they are refugees, like you and me. Being a refugee, we came to realize, is actually a state of mind. A state of being.

You seek refuge in your spouse, in your partner, in your mother, in your father, in your home, in your child, in your friend, in your country, in the ocean, in the darkness of the deafening silence, in the memories of a bygone time, in love, in the name of God. You seek refuge from whatever and whoever is pursuing you in whatever and whoever you trust.

Becoming a refugee in Jordan is not very different from becoming one anywhere else in the world. Displacement. War. Terror. Torture. Captivity. Abuse. Enslavement. These are some of the many aspects of injustice and persecution experienced by refugees across time and place. One common experience these heroic Syrian women share with you is betrayal. Betrayal can be on the individual or the national level. It does not necessarily have to be associated with only friends, spouses, family, coworkers, or neighbors. For decades, Syrians have been betrayed by their leader, by the very leader who took an oath of office to protect them and their children and families. They had no say when it came to elections. Everybody knew who the president would be. Everybody knew whom to vote for. Everybody knew the game is too old and the citizens too obedient. The usual state of affairs. The usual crowds. Some faint fuss in the background, quickly disappearing behind the festive noise of renewing trust in the leader to lead the country to decades of progress and better lives for his children. For his sheep. The ultimate exercise of force, violence, and treason against the very people he ought to serve.

This is betrayal in its most fascinating manifestations. Not behind closed doors. Not in dark, smoky hallways. Not in polished parliament auditoriums. Not in prison cells sealed with the dried blood of generations of men, women, and children who died believing in something. Not for them, not for their children, but for those Syrians who may live to see the sun of freedom shine on whatever beating hearts have remained. Not behind TV screens beating against the lenses of eyes older than history watching the lives of their children flushed away in front of them, having no choice but to smile back at their usurper, their executioner, their rapist, while playing along in the game of life. Performing their dull role in the farce in which animals, plants, and anything with a glimmer of life is doomed to ruin. Serving a life sentence for themselves and their offspring. If it is not bad enough for an innocent soul to serve a life sentence as a slave in a prison, those you will call your children will be destined to serve long before they are conceived.

The human race never disappoints in showing how far one can go in betraying another. Politicians are not the only gifted traitors among us. Every one of us can experience betrayal, as well as exercise it. Few humans are spared the taste of betrayal. Syrians, like the people of several other nations, have been betrayed by politicians, at home and at large. They have been betrayed by so many of us. By those who rallied for freedom and dignity and humanity for all. Many of us are privileged to breathe freely, to wake up every morning and go to bed every night without questioning what it feels like to be free. We have gotten so accustomed to freedom that we take it for granted. Of course, there is nothing wrong with being free. On the contrary, we live to guard freedom in the land of the free, and our men and women certainly pay a hefty price to guarantee us our freedom and peace. However, we have grown so comfortable that we no longer deem the lives of others worthy. We, too, are accomplices in the heinous crimes and genocides taking place thousands of miles away from our warm, beautiful homes. Do not turn a blind eye to what is happening right in front of you. Do not pretend not to have seen something real by changing the TV channel. Do not treat yourself and your children to a new release of *The Hunger Games* in the most luxurious theater in town when the real hunger games and wars are happening right now right there. Just because a wrong does not involve a family member, an acquaintance, or someone with a passport from the same country does not mean that it does not matter to you. Do not numb your senses to spare yourself a traumatic experience you would rather do without. Do not shy away from taking the first step in standing with those persecuted by others.

Now that you can choose to know, choose to know. Choose to say something, to do something. Do not bury your head in the sand and tell yourself it is not your problem. Because it is be your problem. Serve humanity by not serving evil. There are those at the top of the pyramid, and there are those who serve them and carry out their orders. There will always be those who are thrown into the fire so long as those higher up on the pyramid have no regard for their fellow beings. And then there are the watchers, those who watch until they become numb. These are the accomplices. They see. They know. They choose to turn a blind eye. Do not be one of them. Choose to raise your voice. Choose to listen. Allow yourself to feel for others. Retain your human qualities. Otherwise, you, too, will have blood on your hands.

Betrayal is silence in the face of injustice. It is a voluntary choice of slavery, of spiritual death. Syria is burning. Syrians are burning. Join the fight to rescue humanity before it is doomed to annihilation. Seek the truth. Serve the truth. Be part of something bigger than yourself, something far from your personal aspirations. War has never solved a problem but only created many new ones.

The chapters that follow provide an opportunity to listen. To know. To think. To reevaluate life as we know it. Heroic Syrian women have shared a small piece of their lives with you. A glimmer of light will spark only when those claiming to be free in the land of the free act free.

CHAPTER 1

A Chance to Listen

Permit to Visit

When al-Zaatari Camp opened in Jordan in July 2012, it made international headlines. Jordan's reputation as a moderate nation encouraged interest in the newly expanding regional conflict. Soon media outlets, reporters, government officials, and nongovernmental organizations (NGOs) started visiting the camp. Then came the celebrities, like Angelina Jolie and Janet Jackson. These high-profile visits helped draw global attention to the ordeal of Syrian refugees. The eyes of the world were on this place.

On the surface, al-Zaatari appeared exemplary in comparison to other refugee camps in the region. The tents in which refugees were initially housed were quickly replaced with mobile shelters called caravans. These new housing units were made of metal and provided much better protection from the elements. They looked like large shipping containers with small windows. Al-Zaatari also had other things that are usually slow to arrive at refugee camps. There was electricity, and there was water. There were health clinics, schools, soccer fields, playgrounds, small shops, hair salons, bakeries, and even wedding gown shops. The list went on and on. Life sounded too good to be true for a camp.

There was a missing piece. *What is it?* we wondered.

The only people who could answer this were the camp's residents. So we set out to visit the camp, but we promptly realized it was not so simple. We learned we needed an official permit. Going into the camp without an official permit would be risky. Why were things so complicated? Were they hiding something?

The official narrative was that the camp was open to international media, journalists, and really anyone who wanted to visit. The official narrative was that there was nothing going on in secret. Many problems were in need of solutions in the camp. But it was all out in the open. And, to be fair, other researchers, journalists, documentary filmmakers, NGOs, and officials were regularly visiting the camp. But we needed to put the official narrative to the test.

And thus began our journey to secure an official permit to enter the camp and speak to women there.

After several attempts to reach the right person, we learned it would be best to request the permit from the highest possible authority. At the time, that person was Major General Dr. Waddah Humoud, director of the Department of Refugee Affairs. He was in charge of all Syrian refugee camps in the country. We asked for an appointment and were surprised to receive a quick and positive response.

We left in the early morning hours for our meeting with Major General Humoud. We arrived a bit early at his office in Amman and waited anxiously, thinking of what questions to ask. Major General Humoud was a busy man; visitors and officers constantly went in and out of his office. When we were finally admitted, he welcomed us with a smile, although it was clear that he was managing difficult issues at the national level. His cell phone and office phone rang throughout our meeting, and people repeatedly interrupted our discussion.

We explained what we wanted to do in the camp, and Major General Humoud was very receptive. He shared with us the latest official statistics concerning Syrian refugee affairs in Jordan. He described the latest technology the Jordanian government was using to manage refugee data, including biometric tools to ensure refugees have official IDs and . . . "It's for my shepherd!" came a shout from the back of the office.

We looked behind us, surprised not at the interruption but at the words that had been uttered. An old man was approaching, accompanied by an embarrassed officer who had been trying to keep him outside. The man greeted us and apologized for interrupting our meeting. Humoud, not at all surprised by the interruption, allowed the man to make his request. He seemed accustomed to constant, sometimes bizarre, requests.

The man was from a local tribe and owned a large number of cattle. He had hired a Syrian refugee as shepherd, but the refugee's wife needed to renew her expired papers. He needed Hamoud's permission to expedite the process so that the shepherd's wife could remain in the country legally. The major general welcomed him and listened to the man's stream of demands with patience.

This transition from biometric eye-print technology to a local tribesman making a request on behalf of a shepherd's wife was unexpected. But moments such as this encapsulate the struggle of a country striving to change its old ways while also supporting hundreds of thousands of refugees.

By the end of the visit, Major General Humoud assured us our request to visit the camp would be granted. Sure enough, the permit arrived a few days later in a sealed envelope. We started planning the logistics of our visits to the camp.

Our small black Hyundai, with its 1.2-liter engine, was hardly prepared for the journey. As we drove down Baghdad International Highway under the scorching sun, the engine started to overheat. It took us about an hour to reach al-Zaatari Camp from Irbid. The camp was located in Mafraq Governorate, just a short stretch off the highway.

We arrived to find that there were no trees there, no plants or grass, nothing that even resembled green. Instead, we faced an endless stretch of sand. It washed everything with a pale yellow tint, even the soulless white caravans the UN had provided. Everything muddled together until the sand seemed like the only constant physical reality.

As we drove into the camp, we saw women and children gathering around large water tanks and filling water bottles, buckets, and gallon containers. Each water tank was raised on a foundation of cinderblocks. Small children passed us, pushing wheelbarrows many times their weight. Since the refugees had no cars, wheelbarrows had become a valuable possession in the camp. They were used to transfer everything from water to furniture to small children.

We drove straight to the headquarters to speak to the camp director. Along the way, we saw young men walking aimlessly in the burning heat. Children chased our car in curiosity, some raising their hands in the peace sign.

We explained our plans in a brief conversation with the director. Waed would visit the caravans and speak to the women. That way, the women would have the chance to speak more comfortably, without the presence of men. Meanwhile, Muhammad would speak to members of a few NGOs in the camp. A female police officer would accompany Waed and guide her through the camp's districts. Everything had gone as planned thus far, so the next episode came as a complete surprise.

An Attempt to Silence
Narrated by Waed

When the police officer first introduced herself, it crossed my mind that she seemed upset with this assignment. I quickly shook off that idea. *How silly,* I thought, *she's just doing her job.* The camp director delivered some last instructions to her, and then the officer asked me to come to her office. I obliged.

To my surprise, that office visit quickly turned into a long series of questions. She was skeptical of the permit we had obtained, but she asked for it so that she could make copies. I then sat there for at least an hour as she looked at her computer monitor and made phone calls.

She continued questioning me from behind her computer screen. I had not expected such treatment, but I answered all her questions. She addressed me only once, to volunteer her opinion of Syrian refugees in the country: "You know they are now letting Syrian kids into my daughter's private school? They don't even have to pay. It's all covered for them. They're filthy and full of diseases. I don't pay all that money every year so my children can share the same school with them."

Eventually she returned to her interrogation. "Why are you doing this? For whom? What are your plans and intentions?" And then it hit me. I came here to interview the refugee women, but now I was the one being interviewed.

The questions slowly morphed into veiled threats: "You have to be careful about what you write. Every word will be read. You are being watched, so be careful." I tried to answer each question respectfully, but it was hard to ignore the hostility. One worrisome thought occupied my mind the whole time: *If she is treating me this way, how is she treating the refugees, whom she just called all these horrible names?*

"Why do you want to talk to these women? They are liars. Don't talk to them. They never have enough. They only take and complain. Come, I will show you some better people to talk to," she said. I explained that the whole point of our visit was to listen to these women and learn about their experiences from them, not from officials in the camp. But she was adamant.

She dragged me through the offices of several governmental and nongovernmental organizations. At each stop, she led me to employees who raved about the "better than you would expect" conditions in the camp. "They live for free." "They have playgrounds!" "It's a five-star camp!" "This is better than what they had back home." As we walked from room to room, the officer lectured me further on how ungrateful Syrian refugees were.

I decided to put an end to this game. The camp director had clearly instructed her to facilitate our mission. I told her I would talk to the Syrian women now, or I would return to the camp's headquarters to file a complaint. Reluctantly, she agreed.

She still did not do it. Instead, I found myself in an NGO office that hired Syrian women. The officer said, "Here are good examples of women who are employed here." *Oh, for heaven's sake! Do I just burst out of the room?* I thought. It was too late. I was already standing in a circle of chairs occupied by women employees. So I decided to take this as an opportunity to introduce myself. I explained the nature of my research, interview ethics, and the women's right to decline or participate in the conversation. I explained that I would not be asking questions since the officer refused to leave the room, but I would instead like to chat about anything of their choice. That earned me a threatening stare from the officer.

To my surprise, most of the women ignored the officer. And so the conversation covered mundane, everyday things . . . until it did not. One of the women was simply complaining about the difficulty of day-to-day life when the officer decided to interrupt her. But that was a big mistake.

The woman proceeded to berate the officer: "Things are not going to get any worse than they are. No, the situation here is not ideal, as you claim. I had a great life back in Syria that you can't steal from me. I am only here because the war forced me to be here. I don't want your money or your caravan. I wish I could leave today, before tomorrow." She reminded the officer that she, too, is a human being and that this life at the camp was nothing but a temporary stage she was forced to go through. She knew it would end sooner rather than later. This strong woman spoke fluently and intelligently about the challenges faced by refugees at the camp.

The officer could not believe she was being undermined, but the woman said to her, "Things are not good anyway, and we are not happy." The officer said, "You know we are giving you everything we can." The woman replied, "Thank you, but that does not mean the living conditions are great here. This is what I have."

Still uncomfortable with the presence of the officer, I asked to return to headquarters to meet Muhammad. The officer walked next to me the whole way, ensuring that I did not stray farther into the camp. *Does she really suspect I am planning to sneak off to the caravans?*

I must admit that the very thought of her panicked face was tempting. I wanted to quietly sneak off anywhere, even if just around the corner, to catch a glimpse of that expression.

But before I could act, the officer started ordering a ride back to Irbid for me. She tried to put me on the first bus returning to Irbid. We knew we had to speak to the camp director, but he was gone for the day.

Upon returning to Irbid, we did not know what to think. Was that officer working on orders to disrupt our plans, or was she acting on her own?

We got our answer a few days later when we returned to the camp. The camp director was busy receiving an American convoy visiting al-Zaatari. He still spared a quick minute to learn about our problem. He was surprised to hear about what had happened, and he condemned the officer's behavior. He then gave us his personal phone number. We were to call him immediately should we face any issues.

We later came to learn that the hostile officer was likely motivated not by policy but by her personal disdain for Syrian refugees. Of the many other officers we later met, not one held such animosity toward the camp's residents. We felt that most of them realized the plight of the refugees and empathized with their struggle.

The officer was likely aware she had little authority over the camp's residents. On the contrary, she was expected to work with the refugees—not the other way around.

In its early days, al-Zaatari Camp suffered from lack of security. There were incidents of violence, riots, and theft of food rations and health supplies. Jordanian authorities constantly tried to enforce security in the camp. Things finally started to improve but only after the authorities realized it was more effective to work *with* the refugees instead of trying to manage them. So the authorities enacted the so-called community-based protection approaches that engaged the camp's residents.

We still needed officers to guide us through the districts of the camp, so we were assigned three new officers to help us. The director instructed the three men to take directions from us, accompany us wherever we wanted to go, and remain for as long as we needed them.

The unfortunate early encounter with the officer was probably a blessing in disguise. Our way now cleared, we had a plan: I would speak to the women inside the caravans, and Muhammad would ensure that the men and officers remained outside. We wanted only the women and sometimes their young children to be present during the conversations. Adhering to the institutional review board (IRB) regulations, the presence of men was not an option.

And so began our work.

Keeping the Men Out
Narrated by Muhammad

We all huddled close to each other in the tiny patch of shade. When the temperature is well above 100°F, any small spot with shade is beyond value. In the distance, I saw that one of the officers had stayed in the truck. He had the windows open, and I wondered how he was able to withstand the heat.

The other officer was sitting right next to me. So were six other men representing different generations: three young men in their early twenties, one man in his mid-forties, and two men of at least sixty. In my mind, my most important task was to stop any of them from interrupting the conversation Waed and the women were having. I was determined to keep them with me for as long as necessary.

It was not easy.

Every time a son wanted to check on his mother or a husband wanted to see what was up with his wife, I had to make the conversations more interesting. And then there were the grandfathers. They insisted that we have tea, coffee, or something. It is customary in Arab culture, as a sign of hospitality and generosity, to offer your guests something before they leave. The problem is that they would have to interrupt the women's meeting to make the tea or coffee. No matter how many times I insisted that there was no need for tea, I heard only offers of substitute beverage options: "Coffee? Cola? Chamomile?"

I had to invent conversations. But I also had to stay out of politics because the young men were not comfortable adopting a political position publicly. They did not want others to assume they were fighters in disguise. Who could blame them? When you spend every minute of your life under the rule of the same tyrannical regime, you don't trust friends, let alone strangers. But I digress.

This was not as easy as it sounds. I was sitting in the middle of a refugee camp that was created because of political trouble. It is the reason for the human crisis that was staring me in the face. How did they stay out of politics? Every grain of sand around us smelled of it.

Every time the men got bored, tired, hungry, or anxious, they wanted to check on the women. I had only a few seconds to come up with an enticing question, a captivating dialogue, a bad joke. *Anything* that forced them to remain with me.

As I tried hard to distract them, I ended up striking up awkward conversations with myself. Many of the men were not interested in talking. They were sad and quiet, as if they had lost the desire to do even the slightest thing. A few seemed more talkative. They were upset, but the things they were upset about were not what I expected.

One man issued constant complaints about the topics of the Friday prayer sermons at the camp. Perhaps the suppressed political issues we were all avoiding found their way into more mundane topics.

The young men contributed little to the conversations. Many smoked around the clock. They listened, but they seemed fully immersed in their own world, a world to which I had no access. Strangely enough, Waed had better access to that world. Some of her conversations with the women revealed what these young men's minds might be occupied with. Their mothers, wives, and sisters worried that there was nothing for men in the camp. It seems many of these young men struggled with a lack of purpose. Their families worried that they would sneak back to Syria to fight in the conflict as a desperate measure to find it.

The two officers and I made frequent trips back to the truck. They were quite young. Despite their difficult jobs, they made modest salaries. It seemed they were constantly looking for a way out. They both had families to provide for and children to worry about. One told me he planned to enroll in graduate school. He liked his stable pay, little as it was, but he wanted to make an ambitious move beyond his current job.

The other officer seemed under constant financial stress. Whenever he saw a superior officer, he asked for a *sulfa*, a loan paid back in installments from one's salary. Both officers witnessed how difficult life was inside the camp. They hoped life would get better for the Syrian refugees. But they also understood the limitations of their own power and the challenges of their own lives, whether personal, financial, or otherwise.

We moved around the vast camp for hours in that truck, with the air-conditioner on and the windows open. We drank boiling hot tea inside the truck in the searing heat. These things did not make any sense, but neither did our surroundings.

CHAPTER 2

How It All Started

Syria's Colonial Legacy

Bashar al-Assad's regime might be the most brutal in modern Syria, but it is far from the only one. Authoritarian rulers have battled over the country since its independence. Assad just happened to win. But you don't win a power struggle like this without being a special kind of brutal. And the Assad regime was just that.

It is not only Syria that has suffered these irredeemable tyrants. It is a regional problem. Libya had Gaddafi, who ruled for forty-two years. Egypt had Mubarak, who was president for thirty years. Both make the rule of Tunisia's Ben Ali seem short at a mere twenty-four years.

It is also a consistent problem. Many tyrannical regimes remain in power today. Why this is the case is a subject of debate. But one thing is clear: European colonial powers left many Arab countries in disarray, with no democratic systems or structures in place to develop. European colonialists divided Arab countries and drew new borders. They established states that had not existed before, even some that seemed to have no business existing—at least not as independent, modern states.

But sometimes that was the point: to create small, oil-rich states that would always submit to Western support, Western technology, and Western businesses and corporations. States that would always need Western dominance.

The very purpose of colonization is not to help develop modern independent states but to maintain power. European colonialists sought power, so they competed for spheres of influence. They competed to control the region, with its lucrative natural resources and strategic location.

Colonialists crave power, so they leave only after establishing dependency. That way colonized countries remain reliant on them long after their departure. This is hegemony, basically domination by consent. Colonization is always about the interests of colonialist powers; the interests of the native population are not a priority.

Modern colonization had an immense effect on the region. Syrian cities such as Damascus and Aleppo have a history that dates back centuries. Damascus is as much as twelve thousand years old and is widely believed to be the oldest continuously inhabited city in the world. But modern-day Syria, with its current borders, has existed for a fraction of that time.

It all started with a secret deal between the French and the British. The Ottoman Empire was collapsing, and the vast territories it was leaving behind were up for grabs. So the two European powers divided the territories between themselves. Greater Syria is one of these areas, but so are parts of Lebanon, Jordan, Iraq, Israel, and the Palestinian territories. Neither the French nor the British like words such as *invasion* or *colonialism*, so they refer to their control of these nations as a *mandate*.

The French got Syria in the deal. They invaded the country in 1920. For years, they systematically bombarded Syrian cities and used violence against its people. Under their rule, animosity between religious and ethnic groups grew. The French constantly played minorities and religious sects against one another. They actively encouraged religious divisions. They even relocated whole populations to change the country's demography in their favor.

The Rise of a New Global Power

As European powers were preparing to leave, the US role in the region was growing. With the end of World War II, the United States became the major global power. Its only rival was another victor in the war, the Soviet Union. The Middle East became a place where this power struggle was on full display.

US policy makers were concerned that the region would become communist and believed that only authoritarian regimes could resist Soviet influence. American foreign policy in the Middle East developed clear, publicly announced objectives that revealed the country's interest in the region.

The United States wanted a reliable, uninterrupted supply of oil from the Middle East. So it needed stable pro-Western governments. These governments did not have to be democratic, but they had to resist Soviet influence. This is where authoritarian regimes shine: they are able to reliably deliver these goals. As a result, the United States has supported autocrats and a host of kings, emirs, and military officers who have seized power in the Middle East.

US allies in Europe have similar goals in the region, goals they pursue no matter the cost. If the lack of democratic progress is the price of maintaining control, so be it.

History shows that democracy quickly becomes dispensable if it stands in the way of US interests. Some cases, like that of Iran, might even be surprising. In the early 1950s, Mohammad Mosaddegh became Iran's prime minister. He was the head of a democratically elected government, so the country was perhaps on a path toward a stronger democracy. There was just one problem: Mosaddegh did not like British control of the Iranian oil industry, which had been the case since 1913. He believed it was time for the Iranian people to reclaim their natural resources and developed an audacious plan to nationalize the Iranian oil industry. The United States and the United Kingdom could not let this happen, so they helped orchestrate a military coup in 1953 to overthrow Mosaddegh's government. This put an end to Iran's move toward democracy. Iran is just one of many cases of Western intervention in the politics of the region.

Syria is another. Within three years of the departure of the French, the United States supported the first military coup in modern Syrian history. The coup overthrew the country's democratically elected government. It was also the first military coup in the Arab world after World War II. It was a sign of the growing power and influence of the United States in the region.

Government change is not uncommon in the region, but Syria's case is severe. After its independence, the country witnessed a long period of political instability and external interference. Military coups became all too frequent, occurring in 1949, 1954, 1961, 1963, and 1966. Each year, it seemed, a new president was overthrown, another constitution drafted, or a different cabinet introduced. At one point, Syria unified with Egypt to form a new country, one that lasted for only three years.

The Assad Regimes

In 1970, Syria's history recorded one more change. A young military officer named Hafez al-Assad executed a military coup. The young man was minister of defense at the time. He was also the father of Syria's current leader, Bashar al-Assad.

This time there was no more government change, no new presidents or shifts in leadership. Assad consolidated his control of the country, calling his rise to power the Corrective Movement. His regime claimed it would bring unity and equality to the country.

Within a year, Assad was confirmed as president for a seven-year term, and a new phase in Syria's history began. After eighteen presidents and countless military coups and power grabs, the same family would rule Syria until today. Over nearly a half century, Syria witnessed only two presidents: Hafez al-Assad and Bashar al-Assad.

The Assad regime achieved what had for long seemed impossible: undisputed control of the country. The regime would need to take extreme measures to control such a large and diverse nation as Syria, with its turbulent history. It would take brutal force—and a lot of it. But the Assad regime was prepared. It would soon reveal its true colors.

Hafez al-Assad's top priority on seizing power was simple: keep it. From his first day in power, he acted ruthlessly to destroy all opposition. Assad made it clear that Syrians had two choices. They could either support his regime or stand against it. Each choice came with its own set of consequences, and Syrians had to choose very carefully. Supporting Assad would be the clear, wise choice.

And if someone failed to make the wise choice? Anything was on the table. Torture, kidnapping, imprisonment, and death became daily occurrences. It was common for people to "disappear" in Syrian prisons. The inmate's file could not be found, the family might be told. If lucky, the missing inmate might have received a secret burial in an unmarked grave at three o'clock in the morning. After all, what would Assad be if not a merciful leader? It is true that the burial would proceed in complete silence and only a handful of family members would be allowed. It is true that details of that night would never be spoken of again. But at least the family was granted one last look at their loved one.

And then there were acts of mass violence. These revealed how far Hafez was willing to go to maintain control of the country. In 1982, Hafez al-Assad responded to a popular uprising by besieging the city of Hama. His forces leveled entire neighborhoods, killing nearly twenty thousand residents. This would later be known as the Hama Massacre.

Assad used other, sly tactics. Syria is a diverse country with many religious and ethnic groups. What would someone like Assad do with this diversity other than turn it to his favor?

Assad was an Alawite, a member of a religious minority connected to Shia Islam. On the surface he claimed a secular ideology, but in reality his regime thrived on sectarian divisions. The purpose? To give Alawites complete dominance as the country's ruling class.

The Alawites controlled the intelligence forces. They controlled the security forces. They enjoyed preferential treatment but all for a price: unquestioned loyalty. Assad, in turn, ensured that any threats to his position were perceived as threats to the Alawite minority itself.

Not all Alawites benefited from the regime, at least not at this large scale. Some Alawite villages, small towns, and neighborhoods—poor and vulnerable communities—received little government attention. Their proudest benefit from the regime may have been a low-ranking military position for a firstborn son. His pay would be peanuts. But peanuts are better than nothing.

In exchange, the Alawites were loyal to Assad. The alternative, they were told, was no less than revenge extermination at the hands of other groups should his regime collapse. For thirty years, Hafez al-Assad was the absolute leader of Syria. It seemed there was little anyone could do to undermine his authority.

The scale of Assad's control over the country was revealed on his death. When he died in 2000, his son Bashar was ready to assume power. But there was a problem. One had to be at least forty years old to be eligible for the presidency. Bashar was too young. In twenty-nine years, his father was confident enough that he did not change that rule. It took only a few hours for the parliament to amend the constitution, however. The minimum age of the president was lowered to thirty-four, Bashar's age at the time. And as if this was not enough to show the Assad regime's control of the country, Bashar ran unopposed. Other candidates were prohibited.

Bashar won a mere 97.3 percent of the vote, less than his father received when he also ran unopposed a year earlier. Who needs more candidates when reportedly 100 percent of the Syrian people would vote for him? Bashar used these sham elections to claim he represented the will of the people, a claim that was far from reality. He was confident that he would keep his position for the long run. His regime, like his father's, became a monarchical presidency. He ruled like a king, one who would only leave office on death. He joined a group of authoritarian regimes that claim democratic rule but are in fact rulers for life.

As expected, Bashar followed in his father's footsteps. Under his rule, groups affiliated with the regime ravaged the country. They commited shameful acts of violence with few or no consequences. People talked about regime loyalists driving to local high schools and forcing girls into their cars, only to return them days later to their families.

These were not isolated incidents: Bashar's regime exercised systematic violence against the population. Intelligence and security forces had unrestricted authority to maintain civil obedience. They were to do so at any expense.

Bashar showed a new level of brutality when the Syrian uprising erupted. He once again proved his regime was willing to annihilate whatever stood in its way. As the world watched, Bashar used weapons of mass destruction against his own people, killing thousands of men, women, and children.

Bashar also continued his father's claim of fighting imperialist interests in the region. He established strong relationships with powerful allies: Iran, Hezbollah, and Russia. He gave these foreign forces unrestricted access to the country's resources. Russian and Iranian companies were granted contracts worth billions of dollars.

These allies soon proved indispensable to the regime. When the Syrian conflict escalated, they sped full-force to the rescue. With them, they brought immense financial and military power. They would become the reason for the regime's survival.

For many, the name Mohamed Bouazizi might not be meaningful. Most people outside the Arab world have never heard it. And why should they? After all, Bouazizi was a modest street vendor who grew up in a small Tunisian village.

At only twenty-six, Bouazizi had already lived a hard life. He had worked since he was a child to support his mother and six siblings. Each day, he would fill his wheelbarrow with fruits and vegetables and head to the busy streets. At the time, his biggest dream was to rent a pickup truck. But until then, he made do with a wheelbarrow. It was his only means of making a living.

In the grand scheme of things, Mohamed Bouazizi was a nobody. But in 2010, Bouazizi did something that changed the course of history. The cost would be no less profound.

Local police officers had been harassing Bouazizi for years. One morning they confiscated his wheelbarrow. Although they could have been bribed, Bouazizi did not have enough money. Tunisia was suffering under a corrupt and deeply unfair political system led by a tyrannical president. What Bouazizi experienced was not out of the ordinary. Bouazizi was outraged, but he could not find a way out.

Bouazizi was already in debt.

Bouazizi had applied for countless jobs but was not hired.

Bouazizi tried to join the army but was rejected.

Bouazizi was hurt and unable to stand this injustice.

Bouazizi set himself on fire in protest.

. . .

Bouazizi died eighteen days later.

Bouazizi.

Bouazizi started a wave of uprisings against the regime. The people protested unemployment, widespread corruption, and political cruelty. The uprisings toppled the country's dictator in less than a month. Then they toppled Egypt's president. Then Libya's. In the course of the next few years, virtually every Arab country felt the consequences of Bouazizi's act—from complete regime change to civil disobedience to, in the case of Syria, a catastrophic civil war.

Bouazizi became a symbol of protest and freedom in the Arab world.

It was January, and Bashar al-Assad was confident of his grip on Syria. In March, demonstrations began. Assad ordered his secret police and intelligence forces to be ruthless. But the demonstrations grew.

Near the southern town of Daraa, the body of thirteen-year-old Hamza Al-Khateeb was returned to his family. Hamza was accused of taking part in a small protest against Assad. He had been captured by the notorious Air Force Intelligence, the regime's cruelest and most violent security force. The regime wanted to make an example of Hamza, warning Syrians that defiance is unforgivable. Hamza was executed in cold blood, but his family was shocked when they received his body. It had gunshot wounds but also showed signs of horrific torture: his jaw, neck, and both kneecaps were crushed, and he had numerous burns, including the marks of stubbed-out cigarettes. And, as if death and torture were not enough, Hamza's severed genitals were sent with his body.

Hamza symbolizes the incomprehensible cruelty of the Assad regime. It is a regime that exploits children's fragility because the more heinous the crime, the greater the fear instilled in the hearts of citizens. Hamza was only one of many innocent children who lost their lives to the crisis.

Later that year, Bashar al-Assad denied knowing about Hamza. As expected, he rejected all accusations of human rights violations, demanding documents to prove that his forces had committed crimes. Assad described protesters as terrorists and drug smugglers. He insisted that he had the full support of the Syrian people.

The Syrian uprising continued, and Assad began to lose control of the country. He turned to sectarianism for its survival. He asked for the support of Shia-majority Iran and its ally in Lebanon, Hezbollah. He used the Sunni-dominated opposition as a way to appeal for support.

Soon Iran poured its vast resources and regional influence into helping Assad. Military and financial aid arrived. Army generals helped Assad's forces on the ground. Large numbers of militia fighters joined the fight, many in defense of their devout religious beliefs. Hezbollah sent its highly trained troops to fight for the regime. They had been hardened by multiple wars with Israel.

Sunni-dominated Saudi Arabia increased its support for the opposition to combat Iran, its regional rival. US special forces offered support and training to opposition fighters. Other countries joined the fight, supporting different factions with arms and finances.

A new, cruel jihadist force entered the conflict under the name Islamic State of Iraq and the Levant (ISIS). The group exploited the power vacuum left by the Iraq War to gain control over large areas in Syria and Iraq. At one point, ISIS held territory that is home to millions of residents.

It seemed that the regime was destined to fall. It was only a matter of time.

Assad began to use extreme measures. His regime launched a deadly chemical attack against opposition-held suburbs near Damascus, killing 1,429 people, including 426 children. Images and videos of the attack shocked the world. Another chemical attack against the town of Khan Shaykhun killed and injured hundreds.

Russia entered the war. It had long supported Assad with arms and training, but now it conducted regular airstrikes against the opposition. Russian officials claimed they were targeting ISIS, but the opposition and civilian casualties prove otherwise. Rebel fighters struggled to respond to Russia's airstrikes.

Assad's allies proved reliable, and things finally started to shift in his favor. By early 2018, Assad regained control of most of the country.

The Human Cost of the Crisis

The Assad regime continues to act with impunity. Assad's sole purpose is to maintain power, regardless of the human cost. Nearly half a million Syrians—most of them civilians—have lost their lives. When the fighting intensified, entire populations were forced to flee the country. More than 5.3 million Syrian refugees have been displaced due to the crisis. While some have sought safety in Europe, Syria's neighbors host the majority of refugees. Turkey alone hosts 3.1 million registered Syrian refugees. The actual numbers of displaced Syrians around the world are higher. Many Syrians are migrant laborers who have not registered as refugees. Jordan, for example, hosts 1.2 million Syrians, twice the number of registered refugees in the country.

But Jordan has a history with refugees. After two wars with Israel, Palestinian refugees by the thousands fled for their lives and had to be resettled in refugee camps in Jordan. Many still live there today. Palestinians make up an estimated half of the country's population as a result.

The Jordanian government now worries that Syrian refugee camps will become part of a permanent resettlement. It sees shifts in population as a threat to the country's delicate economic and demographic balance. When the Syrian crisis started, Jordan's economy was already struggling. Unlike its gulf neighbors, Jordan has no oil. Its problems have been mounting since the Iraq War. The country's national debt is skyrocketing. Instability in the region is killing tourism, an essential source of revenue in such a small country.

Yet another crisis is now curtailing its trade and transport industries. Real estate prices are escalating, and the already stressed job market is getting worse. Parts of the country are witnessing a severe increase in rents. Education, too, is suffering major problems. Public schools are challenged by deteriorating infrastructure and inexperienced teachers.

Meanwhile, the cost of providing electrical power to refugee camps grows, threatening disruption of the service to these vulnerable communities. Al-Zaatari Camp has become Jordan's fourth-largest city. With nearly eighty thousand residents, it is also the largest Syrian refugee camp in the world.

Slowly, the situation has begun to improve. The United Nations and more than 240 NGOs are offering much-needed help. Infant mortality rates in refugee camps have dropped below the average. Educational opportunities in al-Zaatari also have begun to improve. School enrollment rates have increased, and new facilities have been built. A major improvement in security has allowed equal access to education for girls.

Jordan has constructed a new solar plant and connected it to the national grid, saving $1.5 million each year while reducing emissions by thousands of tons. Humble business opportunities have grown. The camp has developed an informal market with thousands of shops and businesses owned by refugees.

Despite these improvements, life continues to be extremely hard for Syrian refugees. This is only the beginning of a long path to recovery.

CHAPTER 3

Reaching the Camp

Race against Time
Umm Badr

It was a cold November night when a stranger knocked on our door. Scared, I ran and shouted, "Who is there?" The stranger replied, "It is me, Abu Omar. I am here for one minute. Can you open the door quickly, please?" I said, "No, I cannot; my husband is not home. What do you want?" He said, "Just open the door. I have news about your husband." I was scared because my husband was at work, and the sentence *I have news about your husband* is never the beginning of a happy story. At least not during war. Without hesitation, I opened the door. I said, "What happened to my husband? Did the army take him? Please tell me what is going on."

Abu Omar replied, "Unfortunately, they took him from his work. We do not know where he is. I work with him. They almost took me, too. But I have nothing to do with the regime, so they let me go. Your husband is in trouble. We cannot do anything now. Only God can help. You can tell his family he is gone. I have to leave right away. Remember, if anyone asks: you have neither seen nor known me. Peace be with you."

Abu Omar disappeared. I fainted. I could not think of anything other than my husband. I looked for my daughter, Hana. She was playing in her bedroom. I thought of Ali's parents, especially his ailing father and mother. I felt sick to my stomach as I stood up to reach the phone. I called his sister and told her the news. She did not say a word. She came running to our apartment right away. I took my daughter, and the three of us left for my in-laws' house. I kept praying to God to give me power to share the news with his parents.

I moved out of our house after two days and alternated between my family's and my in-laws' houses until more news about my husband was available. I was worried. I did not know what he was going through. But I was sure the army was torturing him. I wished I could reach him and tell him how much I loved him. I thought of his mother. Two of her children were now in prison. I do not know how she could handle it. I thought to myself, *War is hell. We have to get away from hell.*

War is cruel, too.

Children are the immediate victims. How could I convince my daughter we had to stay in town? Every time the soldiers entered the house to check if we were hiding protesters, she hid under the couch. She hates these soldiers. My sisters and I used to watch them training in the morning; we used to enjoy seeing them wearing their army uniforms. Now we hated seeing them. We cursed them. Hana was so scared the last time a soldier came close to her. I saw fear in her eyes. He came closer and said to me, "Is she okay? Why is she scared?" I said, "Oh no, she is not scared. She is happy to see you. She is sleepy, that's all." God damn it. How dared he? Of course she was scared. Soldiers carrying rifles is a scary scene. I had to smile every time they looked at me. I hate them. I used to love them.

After war, something changed about the way I saw the army soldiers. I could not believe they were Syrians. They were no longer the human beings I used to see before war. Something changed in their eyes. They were the same soldiers we wished would pass by our house in the morning. Now Hana cannot forget them. She asked that we move to another town. She did not know it was dangerous to move from house to house, let alone from town to town. We were lucky we were still alive. I decided I was going nowhere until Ali was out of prison. I convinced myself he would be back. I refused to entertain the idea of his death, at least for the time being.

Hana slept next to me at my parents' house. I would get close to her and hold her tight. She reminds me of her dad. She used to be his soulmate. I knew he missed her a lot. *He must be dreaming of her laughter*, I thought. I hoped he was not worried about us. I hoped he knew we were safe. I knew he was very worried about us. I lied to Hana: I said her father was on a trip and would be back in a few days. But what could I have said to her? She is too young to know what war is. I had to lie to her. I know it won't be the last time I do. *Forgive me, Hana*, my eyes told hers.

The next morning, I was drinking tea with my mother. We were expecting news about Ali. No news. No one knew where he was. I was not sure he was alive. Some women said he might be dead. I could not think about that possibility. I could not handle his imprisonment, let alone his death.

And what do I do with our little secret? I thought. *Should I tell my mother or wait until he is back, so we can tell everybody as we planned? Maybe I should wait. He would prefer me to wait. But what if he won't be back before I am due? Oh no, God, no. I am telling everybody tomorrow. I must do so as soon as possible. This baby is our hope. He is going to come back before the baby is born. I know he will. He promised to go with me to the hospital and be the first to carry the baby and read some Quran. Please keep your promise, Ali.*

A Call from the Dead

After several long months, we had heard no news about Ali except that he was alive. I was sleeping at my parents' house when my phone rang at 2:00 a.m.

"Good evening."

"Good evening, who is there?"

"It is me! Could you not recognize my voice?"

"Who? Ali? Are you serious?"

"Yes, Sarah, it is me. How are you and Hana?"

"Oh my God. How are you? You are alive! We miss you."

"You are pregnant, right!?"

"Yes. It is a boy, Ali."

"Thank God. I missed you."

"I missed you too. How is your health? Where have you been?"

"I am fine."

"Thank God. We have been so worried about you. Are you coming back home?"

"Yes, God willing. Tell Hana I miss her. Tell my parents I will be back. How are they doing?"

"We are okay. Asim has not returned yet. Do you know anything about him?"

"No. How is the town? How is our house?"

"I have not been to our house. I am at your family's house and my parents' house. I was advised to leave our house and not to return. War has come to our town. Soldiers are everywhere. It is terrible."

"War will be over. Do not worry. Take care of Badr and yourself, and Hana of course."

"Badr!"

"Yes!"

"Okay!"

"Okay! Let me go. This is the last time I will call you. I am fine. I will come home soon. Do not worry. I love you."

Within a week, I heard a knock on the door. I was cooking with my mother-in-law. I went to see who it was. I asked, "Who is there?" There was no answer. I thought it was a soldier. I hid behind the door and opened it slowly. A thin, weak man was behind the door. I did not make eye contact. He did not move. I looked at him. I knew these eyes. It was Ali, my husband. He was so different. I could not believe my eyes. He was a broken man. He was pale and thin. He lost a lot of weight. This was a shadow of Ali, not Ali. I screamed, "Ali! Ali! Ali!" He hugged me and cried. I could not cry. I felt so strange. I hugged him back. I could not look again in his eyes.

Ali was very thin. How did he lose all this weight? What did they do to him? He looked like he was starving. His face looked different. I could not explain my feelings about this sudden change. For a moment I wished he had never returned. I felt guilty for thinking this way, but I could not accept the reality. I could not believe my eyes. I never wanted to see him this sick. Perhaps death is easier.

I had forgotten about Hana. I screamed, "Hana! Hana! Baba is here!" Hana was watching us from afar. She did not say a word. He walked toward her. She ran and hid inside. I knew how she was feeling. This was not her baba. This was a stranger. A scary one. I told him she must be in shock. I went to bring her. "Come, Hana, Baba is back, Hana! Would you like Baba to buy you a dress?"

Hana was hiding in another room under the couch. She refused to say a word. I told her she should hug her dad and kiss him. I told her how much he missed her. She did not speak to me. I tried to take her into my arms. She refused.

I left the room and returned to Ali. He was sitting with his parents. They looked sad. I wondered if Ali would ever return home. But he was right in front of me.

I told him that Hana was sleepy and she would talk to him later. He did not comment. We ate and went to sleep. That night, he did not talk to me or touch me.

Ali screamed at night. *Will I ever get used to this new situation?* I wondered. *A stranger is sleeping next to me. We do not talk, yet there is so much to talk about.* I wanted to talk. But I did not feel he was ready. He was in pain. He could not sleep through the night. Hana was sleeping in her grandmother's room for the first time. Ali missed her a lot. But he was in so much pain. It is better that she slept there. She heard him screaming at night. It was a nightmare. I could not sleep. I could not believe Ali was sleeping in the same bed with me. I could not believe he was back.

Was he back?

The Departure: Shutting the Door for Good

The next morning Ali said we needed to move. His family said we needed to go first, and they would follow us. We went to visit my family one last time. He told them they, too, needed to move as soon as possible. They agreed. Someone informed him our town would be attacked soon. I was pregnant and expecting the baby any minute. I asked that we wait. Ali refused. He said it was dangerous to stay.

I did not know where we would be moving. But I did not consider Jordan. I used to make jokes about anyone saying we might have to move to Jordan. *I cannot become a refugee*, I thought. *I will never be. Hana cannot grow up in a refugee camp. And what about Badr? Will he be a refugee baby?*

I felt dizzy. I cried. I prayed we would not move. *I cannot leave, not now.*

Ali said we needed to start packing. We were to fit everything in two bags only. We gathered whatever we could carry of our belongings and left the house. Ali and I could not say our good-byes to our house. It was the saddest moment in my life. I felt we were betraying a family member. Our house meant our life and future to us. We left our memories and happiness behind. We headed toward the unknown. I knew we might never return to the same house. I had to assure Hana that we would return soon. That the house, as well as her stuffed animals and favorite toys, would be waiting for us when we returned. It broke my heart to shut the door for good.

I shut it quietly. It was not possible not to disturb the memories.

Arriving at al-Zaatari

I knew our home would be turned into rubble in a matter of days. I tried to escape from that horrifying image. We carried our heavy hearts and luggage and left. We walked in the dark with hundreds of people. Those we knew and those we did not. We were all lost and scared. The thought of running from bloody death to protect our children kept us going. We agreed it was not the best decision to leave. At that point, it was a matter of life or death.

We started walking, and there were so many people walking with us. Ali was right. A woman told me her husband had received news that the town would be attacked. I was worried about the people we left there. Ali said they were safe now, but they would have to leave soon. I was worried about the baby inside me. About Hana. Hana no longer talked a lot. She would not talk to her dad. She started calling him "my mother's husband." She broke his heart. I wished I had died before I heard her say so. But I understood her struggle. I, too, was feeling lost.

We continued walking. Ali carried the two heavy bags. He was in so much pain. We were still in Syria but close to the Jordanian border. I felt a lot of pain in my back. I sat down to rest. I started to feel contractions. They continued. I asked for help. We were advised to change routes and look for the closest house. We did. We were welcomed by a Syrian family. They shared their house with us. I did not deliver that day. The next morning a midwife came and checked me. She said I would deliver within two hours. She gave me a hot drink and asked me to keep walking. I did.

I delivered that day. My baby, Badr, was very beautiful. He was as beautiful as Hana. As I was giving birth to him, I heard the sounds of bombs falling on the towns close by. I thought I would die. I prayed that Badr would live to make his father happy.

We both lived. Badr was healthy and happy. I was relieved that he and I were safe now. I did not care what happened next.

Ali and Hana were delighted. Hana carried Badr and refused to give him to her father. She gave him to me, and I handed him to Ali. Ali was sad about Hana but happy about Badr. I knew Ali would get better because Badr was there. Badr did not cry often. It was as if he knew life was tough. He did not want to make it worse. Or perhaps he cried a normal amount, but now I was old enough to handle a newborn. He brought hope back to our hearts.

Ali could not sleep at night. I was not sleeping either. We knew we had to leave again soon. We waited two weeks and left. We continued walking. Ali struggled to carry the bags. I felt sorry for him. But I could not help him. I was carrying Badr. I was tired. There were so many people walking with us. Some were escorted by trucks and cars. Some walked and walked. Ali told me that so many people moved to Jordan every day. I felt safer. At least we were not alone. I assured myself we would not be alone in the camp. Those people walking with us would help each other there. And we would return together after this war was over.

We walked and walked and walked toward the border. Children were screaming and crying. We sat and took a break from walking every half hour or so, so the kids could eat some bread and cheese. I had packed bread, cheese, and water, and I gave Hana some every time she was hungry. Ali and I did not eat much. We sat to rest from the heavy weight we were carrying. As we got closer to the Jordanian border, we rested on a hilltop, and Syria was in front of us. We saw lights in the sky and heard the sounds of bombs. It was a very strange feeling. Our people were dying there. We were safe. They were not.

I continued walking while carrying Badr and holding Hana's hand. There were so many people walking with us. We were walking in the middle of a desert, and I was cursing the regime, the rebels, and the war. They made us race against time. I wanted to look back to see Syria on the horizon. I kept going. The thought of what would become of my family in Syria never left my mind. I was walking with a sick husband, an exhausted child, a newborn, and a broken heart.

After arriving at the Jordanian border, we were escorted to a waiting area and then to al-Zaatari Camp. The camp was much worse than what I had imagined. It was the first time I saw a camp. Al-Zaatari was in the middle of the desert. I refused to believe we would live there. I hoped this would be a transitional stage and we would live somewhere else until we returned.

There were no trees. No humans. No water. Nothing.

We entered a tent. We were told it was our new home. Hana cried and refused to talk to us. She wanted her bed and bathroom, but there were only public bathrooms far from our tent. I had to go there a few times a day. It was the dirtiest place I had ever seen. It was also dangerous at night. I went a couple of times with Hana. At the back of my mind were all the rape stories and rumors people talked about. Hana would often change her mind and return when she saw how dirty the bathrooms were.

There were so many people from different towns. I did not want to talk to anyone. I was so tired and sleepless. I was angry, too. I could not accept the new situation. I did not want it. I wanted something better for Hana and Badr. But remembering war made me wish our families would have come here sooner rather than later.

Now . . . I do not mind this life. I will get used to it. I want Hana and Badr alive. Syria is not safe. I hate the soldiers. I lost the husband I knew. I cannot afford to lose my two children, too.

I often think of how the shelling of our town turned it into a cemetery. No one knew what to do; we were in a state of shock. Thousands of women and children hurried to leave after their men left. Some went to fight. Others were arrested. Or got killed. They packed their most important things and left. They had to make a decision and act: there was no time to meditate.

The difference between life and death was mere minutes.

Mothers grabbed their children and ran in the middle of the night. They did not know where to go. They had to leave as fast as possible. Some refused to leave Syria. They went to safer Syrian villages or towns. No one believed the chaos would turn into war. No one wanted to leave for good. But war was creeping quickly everywhere. Rumors turned into reality. Staying meant torture. Death. Horror. The eyes of the Assad regime were following us. Leaving did not mean we were safe. The Assad regime had spies everywhere. In Syria, we were cautious in the streets. In our homes. The Assad regime made us believe it can hear us even in our bedrooms. We filtered everything. The regime ruled through fear.

We left Syria behind us. The shelling lit up the sky. Our hearts were stamped with horror forever.

Chaos

Tents were distributed in al-Zaatari Camp. Chaos filled the place. Children slept on our shoulders and on the ground. People fought over everything. It was a war of survival here, something we had not prepared ourselves for. Thousands of people were arriving every day. The camp officials lost control over the people. We soon learned that gangs started to micromanage the camp. The UN Relief and Works Agency and several other NGOs provided basic help, such as tents and food. But life was extremely hard. We heard of rape cases, and we could not make sense of what was going on. The public bathrooms were disgusting. Sand got in everywhere. It was in our lungs and mouths. Dirt was everywhere. It was in our food and clothes. The water was dirty. Diseases spread.

At some point, I felt that most people had become abusive. Humiliation and desperation made many people mistreat each other. Food was scarce. People were trying to protect their livelihood. Food and diapers were stolen from the NGOs. Several NGO caravans were destroyed. People were angry. They demanded a better life from the camp officials. When their demands were not answered or were not answered immediately, they protested and destroyed the caravans operated by NGOs.

The first few months were extremely hard. We felt humiliated in a country that was not ours. We expected better treatment. We felt the camp officials would not accept for themselves the life we were offered. But we also saw how they were working for us around the clock. There were too many people. Too many problems. It was too much chaos to handle. The camp was a mess.

Life in the camp is much easier now. Although we are not in a war zone, we cannot forget what happened in our country. We could not put the past behind us and live a normal life. War is still near, even after years.

People these days either return to Syria or manage life here. They complain less. Hundreds and hundreds of children were born here. The camp is all they know. They know Syria through the stories they hear from others. Some stories are sad. But some talk is of Syria, the green paradise. Many women, including me, promised to keep Syria alive in our children's minds and hearts through stories. Some women took some of their family photos with them. These were the lucky ones. Many lamented leaving their precious memories behind. Many risked sending a family member back to retrieve boxes of photos. The loss of such a treasure was like the loss of a family member to war. Memories were escaping our heads. This is a scary fact. We did not know if we would ever return, if Syria would ever be the Syria we loved and lived in. Starting to forget the beautiful memories we had was like a death sentence. We did not want our children not to know their homeland. We did not want to have only memories of war and destruction in our minds.

Ali would eat once a day and sleep most of the day in the first few months of our arrival. He did not speak much. He continued to scream at night. His pain did not seem to subside with time. Later, he started to get better. One night, he talked to me. He asked me to scratch his back. I saw scars. So many scars. I did not ask about anything. He seemed like he wanted to say something.

"You must be in so much pain."

"They tortured me so bad. I almost died. I bled every day. I cannot feel my back anymore."

"Goodness. I am so sorry. I cannot see your back. All I can see is scars. Deep wounds."

"They used us as their ashtray. They burned us."

"Syrian soldiers?"

"Yes."

"How many of you were there?"

"Hundreds."

"How old?"

"All ages."

"Did anyone die?"

"Yes. Every day. We were ordered to carry the dead to a separate room. It smelled so bad. They tortured us around the clock. I expected to die next."

"God! I was scared. I did not know what happened to you. No one knew."

"The plague spread in prison. So many men died. I needed to live for you and Hana."

"We were waiting for you every day. I prayed for your safety."

"War is dirty. I wish it never happened. The prison is so dirty. They made us drink from the same cup we used in the bathroom. Animals would refuse to sleep where we used to sleep. They hanged us for days until we thought we were dead. Did you scratch my back?"

"I did."

"Can you do it again?"

"Of course."

"I do not feel anything. Can you use a needle?"

"God, no! Are you crazy? You need to heal."

"I need to feel. I will never heal."

"I am sorry, *habibi* [my love]. I am so sorry."

"I am sorry, too. At least I lived to see you and the kids. Some of my friends and relatives were tortured to death in front of my eyes."

"And your brother? What happened to him?"

"He died. No one knows. I carried his corpse. I died with him right there."

"Oh, my God. Are you serious? Your brother is dead? Your father is waiting for him."

"And he was waiting for me. There is no return. He is in a better place. He would have killed the first soldier he saw in our town had he left prison alive."

"Would you?"

"No."

"You would not?! Why?!"

"You will know later."

"I want to know now. They killed your brother and friends and tortured you."

"You will know later. There are many things that you would prefer not to know."

"I do not understand."

"Neither do I."

His eyes have changed.

During his time in prison Ali lost sight in his right eye. He refused to tell me how. I did not notice until he told me. He said they made him sit on a chair designed to break one's back. They broke his. He could not take on certain jobs in the camp because of his back pain. He was a different person. He was depressed. Whenever he talked about torture and killing in prison, he would stop and say, "Why are we talking about this? What for? Let us talk about something else."

Even these half-stories were useful in some ways; they enabled me to inch closer to understanding his pain. To listen to him. He needed to tell me many things. He could not. He told me a few stories that made me throw up. He made me promise never to tell anyone. I did not. I worked hard to bury them in the back of my brain. I was able to, but he was not.

The look in his eyes has changed, too. He is not a man in his twenties. He has aged fast. He talks, breathes, walks, and thinks like an old man. I asked him if he thought of suicide when he was in prison. He said he tried to commit suicide several times, but his attempts failed. He said he could not take the horror he had been through in prison. He said a father committed suicide after his two sons were hanged in front of him.

He said he was unhappy in al-Zaatari Camp. He insisted we would return to Syria one day. Maybe next year. I said we should not return unless he did not mind seeing his children suffer. He did not answer. He has changed a great deal. With every passing day, he became more nervous and stressed. Hana and Badr helped him get better. Badr was growing very fast. Hana started to become jealous when Ali played with Badr. Like Badr, she started calling him Dad. Whenever Ali gets Badr something, he gets Hana something too.

Twenty Jordanian Dinars a Month

Each person was given twenty Jordanian dinars' worth of coupons. That was not enough. Ali had to find a job. He worked when he could. I brought my jewelry with me from Syria. It was worth three thousand dinars. I insisted that Ali sell it so we can open a business. He said he would open one when he had the money for it. He refused to sell the jewelry he had bought me throughout the years. I did not mind selling it to make our life better. Now that the dust has settled, I am glad he did not.

After countless attempts, Ali secured a stable part-time job in one of the camp stores. He made more money. A family sold us their caravan before they returned to Syria. Someone in Syria sent him money to help with the caravan's purchase. He bought it for four hundred dinars. Our home became bigger.

One day, Ali gave me the best gift ever.

It was a small bathroom. It is not a real bathroom, just a functional one in a covered corner in the caravan. This was the best thing to happen since we arrived.

I no longer had to walk to the public bathrooms. Hana became happier, too. What a relief. We had to use the public bathrooms for a year. Ali also got us a small television. We turn it on when we have electricity. Life started to get better after these major changes.

Ali started to gain weight. He became stronger. But his heart is still broken. The only time I was sure of his happiness was when he played with Hana and Badr. He loves them so much. Our relationship has improved. But it's nothing like the past. It is like living with another person. A stranger I do not blame. I feel his struggle. I do what I can to see him and our children happy. But try as you can. For war has turned his eyes off.

A Toy from Amman

Ali said we should have a third child one day. I said, "I do not think so. Two is enough. We are not in our country, and our lifestyle has changed. We are lucky to raise two kids under such circumstances." He did not comment. He still thinks war will be over and we will return. Truth is, I think we will not return.

Hana hides when she hears a loud sound. She thinks it is a bomb or a shot. He saw her hiding one day. He hugged her. He said we are safe here, so she need not worry. Are we safe here? Is Hana safe here? I doubt it. One can say we are safer here than there. But what is "safety"? How do you measure it? We do not live in a real society. Men are depressed. Money is scarce. Water is not clean. Diseases are spread. I fear for our well-being.

I worry about Hana. She is getting used to life here. She does not want to return. One day we left the camp to go to Amman, and she came with us. When we returned, she went to play with the neighbors' daughter. I overheard them talking.

"Where did you go, Hana?"

"We went to have fun."

"Where?"

"Outside the camp."

"What did you buy?"

"I bought a toy."

"My mother no longer buys me toys like my father used to. I wish he was alive."

"I will tell her to buy you a toy like mine. Do not worry."

"How is it outside the camp? Is it like Syria?"

"No. It is like the camp, but it is cleaner and less crowded."

"I miss Syria."

"I do not. I do not want soldiers to come to our house. Here they cannot come."

"You are right. They cannot come here."

I took one of Hana's old toys and gave it to her friend. Hana did not mind. She has a new toy. The girl was delighted. She was nine or ten years old. Her father died in Syria. His wife struggles now to bring up their children. She has five of them. She can hardly cover their basic needs. It is hard to make ends meet in the camp with a husband. It is harder as a single mother. Most women do not work. Men and male children try to work. They are willing to take on any job. I cannot see myself letting my son, Badr, work. I will save my jewelry to help him open a minimarket when he is a grown-up. I fear the day Badr becomes a young man here. I wonder if the camp will make him a madman. Will he understand that we left to protect him and his sister? Will he get married here one day? Will he take care of us when we are old and useless? Will he still go to school? Will we get old here?

Decision under Threat
Rama

When we first arrived at the camp I could not sleep. The electricity was shut down. I read the Quran often in search of peace. I wanted to do something instead of just lying down all day long and crying.

I could not move from bed. I tried to think of something beyond the camp. I failed. I knew we are not going to return to Syria. We are not going to move to a nearby Jordanian town. I realized we are stuck here. There is no escape from the grim reality outside. At that very moment I thought, *I hate the camp.* I wished we had never had to leave.

Leaving home was a decision taken under threat. We had to think of what's best for our children's safety first. Walking with hundreds of people toward Jordan meant getting closer to safety. We were leaving bombs and death behind us in Syria. Arriving at the camp made me question several things in life. I regretted having children. I wished I had only two kids instead of seven. I looked at them. I looked around me. Barren desert. Angry screams of people fleeing from war to chaos. This was not the future we wanted for them. My neighbor worried about her children. The horrors of war traumatized them. She was thankful to be in the camp, far from war.

We lack the basic elements that make life worth living. We were scared in Syria. We are scared here too. It is dangerous to be in Syria. It is dangerous here too. We were stuck in Syria. We are stuck here. We might have died in Syria. We will eventually die here too.

I hate being reduced to just a refugee. We felt sorry for the Palestinian refugees in Syria and Lebanon. Now we are in a similar situation, or worse. Maybe we should return to Syria and let come what may. My husband knows what is going on in the camp. He prefers not to share it with me. He knows doing so will double his headache. He thinks by himself. War haunts him. He still wants to return. For years, I talked to him and others in the camp about returning. No one seemed interested in discussing anything. I do not want to keep thinking by myself.

If only my husband could work like other men. He is disabled. A broken man. If only I could work. I have brilliant ideas. The lack of opportunity here limits our options. I applied for jobs more times than I can count. I was always told that there are thousands of women waiting to work, just like me. I was told to be patient. The children are growing up, and their demands increase. Life teaches one to be patient. You wait for the end of month to make ends meet. You wait for NGOs to cover electricity bills to have the lights on. You wait on a long waiting list for a potential part-time job. You wait for a miracle to happen. You wait for war to end. You wait for the sake of waiting. You hang on unlimited "ifs" until you are no longer certain of anything. This is what war does to you. This is the scary part.

The camp's administration said the camp's electricity bill was too high due to illegal use. The camp had to wait for international organizations to cover the cost before power could be restored for all residents in the camp. Refugees need electricity. They cannot pay electricity bills. They cannot pay for their food. What happens when you have nine individuals jobless and hopeless in your family? What happens when you live in a small caravan with no privacy? When you can no longer promise your children that it will get better soon? When you think of committing suicide not because you are weak or tired but because you cannot see your children lose their childhood and future in front of you? Because you can no longer help watching their bodies jump in fear during sleep. When you can no longer look in their eyes and be certain that they are still there.

Walking at Night to Jordan

We were told to leave Syria immediately and join the people walking at night toward the Jordanian border. My oldest daughter and son, who were fifteen and seventeen at the time, refused to leave with us. I had to drag them and scream at them. I was paranoid. It was a matter of life or death. I told them it was selfish to stay and that they had to leave for the sake of their younger siblings. They left with us. They refused to talk to me or their father. We have not talked. They respond with short answers of yes or no. They say we ruined their future. I explained that they would have been dead had they stayed in Syria. But they think otherwise. It kills me that they still blame us for leaving. This had an impact on their siblings' relationship with us. They both refused to go to school at the camp. All they do day and night is stare at their father and me.

My daughter Fadwa is beautiful and smart. She does not want to get married at the camp. She says it is inhumane to bring children to life here. They will be refugees before their birth. She is stubborn but wise. Her father and I agreed to respect her wishes with regard to marriage. Stories of marriage and divorce in the camp helped her reach her decision.

When we first arrived at the camp, I hoped life would get better. I hoped we would get used to our new life. It was not that simple. The daily influx of refugees. The conditions of life. The lack of basic human rights. I preferred a dignified death in Syria. As for my children, I blame Assad and his army. They betrayed their people and robbed them of their right to education and dignified life. They made Syrians flee their home country. You gather your children and flee your home. You become a refugee in the desert. You lose all your privileges. Your rights become a privilege. You live to survive war. You draw on hopes to survive the camp. Then comes winter. It slaps you on your face. It shows you how worthless your life is. How much of a failure you are. You see your children tremble from cold. You fail to make them warm. You wish the earth would swallow you at once, so you never have to see that look in their eyes again.

It was our first winter in the camp. Winter in the desert was not nice. It rained a lot. The camp turned into a swamp. You walk in mud and sit on mud. Rain and mud blew our tent away. We live now in a caravan, but the months we spent in that tent were harsh. We did not have a constant supply of electricity or clean water. We walked and stood in lines for hours to get water. It was terrible. It was contaminated. Everything happened so quickly. More and more refugees arrived every day. We could not absorb the shock of what we had to face. If you have witnessed one winter here, you would understand me better. Tents are no good in normal weather conditions. How on earth can humans survive temperatures below freezing in a tent? Tens of tents caught fire. Those who survived the fire were burned. They suffered a lot. Even in caravans, we freeze and wait for the horror to pass with the least loss possible.

Fighting Rain in a Tent

Children and the elderly struggled the most in winter. One night it was raining heavily. It was so cold. We could not deal with the cold. We gathered in one of the corners of the caravan and held each other's hands and arms. Outside we heard children and women wailing. We heard men screaming, asking God to rescue or kill them. To put an end to this. My son kept reading his prayers. My husband made the children promise they would not cry so loud or scream like others. He said there was no use in doing so, and we should get through this hard time. I cried quietly. I felt helpless to keep my children warm from the biting cold. They were trembling in front of my eyes. We were all soaking.

I never thought something like this would happen to us. I blame the entire world for what happened to us. I know people know what is going on in al-Zaatari Camp, but no one cares. Imagine if something like this was happening to Europeans: the world would stop and take notice. But here as Syrians flee Assad, we are subhuman.

Three-Year-Old Boy Nearly Dead in the Biting Cold

Do you see this woman sitting next to you? Her name is Jaseera. She came with three children, and their caravan was no good. One night I heard her scream that her son was dying, and I ran to see what was going on.

Her son, Amjad, was three years old, and he was turning blue. We thought he died in her arms. The other two children were watching, trembling in the cold. They had nothing in the caravan. Nothing but dirt and mud. The children asked me if their brother had died. I ran to his mother. She was hysterical. I did not know what was happening. Amjad was turning blue, and he was not responsive. I took him from her hands and started shaking him. I tried to find out if he was alive or dead. I knew immediate help was not an option on such a cold night. I held him tight and covered his cold body with my scarf. I read the Quran over him and kept caressing his forehead. Suddenly he moved and started sneezing. Life came back to him. I screamed,

"He is well, he is alive! Do not worry!" But his mother could not react in any way. She froze in her spot. Her other children ran closer to their brother.

I had no time for emotions. I gave her Amjad and asked her to go to the camp administration the next morning to make sure the child is okay. She would not let me leave. Jaseera was scared it would happen again. I had to leave to take care of my children. Every time Amjad sees me, he kisses my forehead and thanks me for saving his life. You know, I did not save his life or anything. I tease him and his mother sometimes, but truth be said, God saved him and us all.

The biting cold in a desert tent is not something you want to experience. Children were crying. They were hungry. Parents had to go to great lengths to fetch them something—anything—to eat. We are glad that winter is over. Winter is death. I wish the camp was not in the middle of desert. I wish it was in any other place. All you see around you is desert. It is like everything around you is saying, "You are trapped in this spot, and you will die here." Some tried to escape. The camp police brought them back. It created so much chaos and violence. I do not blame people who try to escape. If I were any good, I would escape. It would at least make me feel like I have tried to resist this trap. To do something. Anything.

Warning Children against Escaping from the Camp

We warned our children against escaping the camp, especially our daughters. It is terrible, of course. I wished my eldest son would forget about us and the camp and escape. I wished he would start a new life in a Jordanian town. Anything but the camp. He is like a flower wilting in front of my eyes every day. I have other children. They are younger than him. He had a future planned. He refused to leave Syria. We insisted that we all leave as a family. No one was to be left behind. It is like he knew better than us. We wanted to save his life. Thinking about it again, I do not think we saved their lives. They are losing the best years of their lives here. Staying in Syria meant a quick, ugly death. Being here is a slow, impending death. The bells of war signaled our doom.

Look at my daughter. Look in her eyes. She has the eyes of a forty-year-old. She was bubbly and happy in Syria. Every day she gets worse. She used to be the most talkative girl in her school; she would not let her father or me finish a conversation without interrupting us. She is intelligent. Now she hardly speaks. She is mad at us. She is sad and miserable. I tried to enroll her in the school here to get her to have friends. She refused. I begged her to go for one day. She went for one day. She never returned to school. She is traumatized like her brother.

We are all in a state of shock. Some of us were able to adapt to living here. There are children who were born here. All they know is the camp. It is their hometown. They hear people talk about war and homeland. They cannot understand a thing. Some of them love the camp because they do not know better. It is sad. I look at them and wonder how happy they would be if they were born in Syria. If they drank clean water. If they had electricity. If they lived like us. They try to play and laugh. I look at them and wonder if they will ever leave this cage and see their real towns and gardens. They will be shocked, but the good kind of shock, you know.

Point of No Return
Fatima

We were sitting in the living room, waiting for news. It started as distant sounds of bombings. Then the bombings escalated. We did not have time to prepare for this. We did not know if war would reach our town. We refused to think about it. The bombings continued nonstop. We ran to the underground cellar. Men, women, and children. All hurried. We covered the children's heads with our bare hands. We worried a bomb would reach them at any minute.

After long hours in the dark, the morning arrived. We left the cellar and went to the house. We picked out a few things and left. We were racing against time. Against a time bomb. We arrived at a neighboring town. We discovered it was attacked and the ones who were not killed left. Nobody was there. We stayed there briefly. This time we evacuated to al-Zaatari Camp. Some families went to Lebanon, some to al-Zaatari, some to other places. We left, carrying nothing but children.

It was not a smooth journey. We left everything behind. Horror made us leave. We could not look back. We were happy to reach the Jordanian border. None of us left home by choice. It was by force. I was never ready to leave home. But I had to walk with the rest of the group. When we arrived at the camp, I saw what I saw. I said, "I want to return to Syria." The camp was not like this, not like it is now. The first year was the hardest. My heart gradually gave up and hope within me faded away. I left my daughter behind in Syria. She got married two months before we left. I was torn between thinking about her and getting by here.

Home is where you spend time with the ones you love.
Home is safety. Home is warmth.
Home is the comfort of your children around you.

My second daughter, Sama, came with us. She got married here. She returned with her husband to Syria. Her husband insisted on returning. We were torn to see her go. We think about her every day. We worry we will hear bad news about her. We pray God will save everyone in Syria.

I have to say, life at the camp now is much better. Imagine leaving the comfort of your home to live in a tent, or even in a caravan like we do now. When we first arrived it was extremely hot. We looked for any shade to sit in to hide from the sun. We lived for two months in the tent, thank God. Now we have water, bathrooms, and electricity. Not long ago it became available from 7:00 p.m. to 5:00 a.m.

My husband and I do not work. The kids cannot work either. I would rather not complain. I do not like to complain. I just say, thank God. My husband's hair became white here. He questions his self-worth day and night. He cannot sit idle, without a job. The children ask for things, but we cannot afford anything. I have two sons and two daughters here. One of the girls is fourteen. Her sisters got married early. She is too young. Why hurry to get married?

I miss my daughters in Syria. I told my husband we need to return to Syria despite the dangers. Then I say to myself, I will destroy my family here if I insist on returning to connect to my family there. My town is not safe. When I call my daughter, I ask her, "How is life?," and she makes me promise not to return. She says it is not safe. I just feel like my daughters are lonely there, and I have to support them. I have to be there for them. And here for the second part of my family.

I hope things change here. I hope life gets better for everybody. People rise every day and make the best of what they have despite the lack of resources. We share an aspiration: opportunities and jobs for all. I saved some money after selling one of our houses in Syria. It helped us the first few months here. People wish for war to end. People want to return to Syria. To their homes. To their families. To their gardens and lives.

I do not wish for anyone to leave home. Sometimes it takes leaving home to appreciate what you had. To wish to be given the choice again.

To choose to remain.

What the Soldiers Did
Maya

Terrorists attacked our town. They broke into our house. I do not know who they were. Soldiers. Or rebels. Or terrorists. They entered and destroyed houses. No one knew who was fighting whom. We heard soldiers screaming behind the front doors. Shots were fired. We refused to open the door. They broke down the doors and the windows. They forced their way into the rooms. They stole our stuff. They threatened to kill anyone who tried to stop them.

We did not know what they wanted. My father and brother were not at home. One of them said I should go with them. I was horrified.

I started screaming and hid behind my mother. It was complete chaos. My mother slapped him. He pushed her. She fell to the ground. My sisters ran to the kitchen and locked the door. I did not know what to do. All I remember is that I screamed. And screamed. They had guns. They pointed their guns at my mother. No neighbors could come close to the house. They knew something wrong was happening at our house. Everyone was scared that the same thing would happen to their family. You do not know what to expect when strangers enter your house. When war broke out, stories of all sorts started reaching the towns one after one.

My father and brother were not at home when the soldiers attacked. That was a blessing. They would have been killed had they been home that particular night. I thought the terrorists would drag me away with them and I would never see my family again. It happened to several girls in my town. The same scenario happened at the home of one of our relatives. The men were shot to death. Daughters and the mother were taken away. It was best to avoid the encounter between men and soldiers.

These terrorists have no religion. I do not remember what Mother said to make them leave. It was a miracle. They destroyed everything and left. One of them said they would return in the morning. My father and brother came back that morning. We all left immediately. We needed to go somewhere, anywhere. We moved to another town until we figured out what to do. People were kind to us. They shared their homes with us. But then that town, too, was attacked. We all had to go to Jordan.

Homes were leveled.

The soldiers said Assad would win.

Even at the cost of burning the country to the ground.

They are burning the country now. He is winning. But I cannot understand. What will remain for him after war ends? Syria is gone. Its people are scattered around the world. No one is winning in this war. Even Assad is losing. He is losing Syria and Syrians. He claims to fight ISIS. But this mess allowed for ISIS to come to being here.

He is responsible for letting them cross the borders. Here in the camp we fear the spies of the regime. We fear they may be listening to what we say to inform the regime. We have to be careful. We try not to talk about Assad or what happened in Syria. If they hear something they do not like, they are able to hurt our relatives in Syria. Or arrest those who return to Syria. Assad's spies lived among us in Syria. They harassed people.

What is the use of talking about what happened in Syria?

Talking will not return Syria. It will not put Assad behind bars. It will only make things worse. Talking hurts. Women may open their hearts. Only to share a fraction.

Call from Hell
Aneesa

My husband was martyred three years ago. My children and I ended up here. May my husband's soul rest in peace. He is in a better place now.

I find living here without a man easier than with a man. Since the war erupted, men, like everyone else, have been through a lot. It is hard not to be impacted by war. War changes people. War destroys people. War takes away your loved ones. It destroys you. It makes you fight for those who remained. I have been watching how people treat each other under pressure. Like any other society, the camp has the good and the bad. Those we used to call strangers have become like relatives now. You have to connect with your community. You cannot say I do not belong here and I do not want to engage with my neighbors. You may say so at the beginning. But as time passes by, you learn to be part of this community despite its defects. Despite your judgment.

Women here are mothers. Wives. Daughters. Sisters. Grandmothers. Aunts. Women. And loving strangers you grow to call family. Divorced, married, single, or widowed. They pave their own way every day and welcome the day with gracious hearts. I have yet to meet a single woman who puts herself first. Women are the symbol of sacrifice. The laughter of children around them is worth the world for them. Making others happy is a woman thing. What do they want? Nothing for themselves. They want others to be happy and safe. Others are an extension of themselves. In seeing their families happy, they find happiness and comfort. They are selfless in every possible way. When men cheat or divorce, women stay for their children. They find something and someone to live for.

I live here by myself with my five children. I have two sons and three daughters. My oldest son is ten years old. After my husband was martyred, we waited a few months and then came here. He was working with a medical team to care for the wounded fighters in the Free Syrian Army. Someone reported him to Assad's forces. They arrested him. Then we were informed of his death.

We used to live in al-Sayyida Zaineb Province. Then the war started. Families started leaving the town. My family left it too. We returned to our town after a while. The war was still going on. We got used to the bombing and shelling. Our house was close to the palace of Assad, the Palace of Conferences.

My husband had a nickname different from his name on the ID. People knew him by his nickname more than by his name. He would go through checkpoints to areas controlled by the Free Syrian Army in order to heal their wounded fighters. My children and I stayed in an area inhabited by Alawis and Shiites and government employees working with the military and security forces. We were neighbors. After the war we believe the majority of them became spies for the government, collecting news about anyone helping the Free Syrian Army. These spies would pretend to sell goods from a cart or take a stroll, and all the while they would be collecting information and spying on people. We learned to keep our mouths shut.

The Call

One day, the Syrian army entered the town and searched the houses for men. Finding none, they left. Women and children left their houses and ran outside. There were no men in the town. All of them escaped. Assad's forces asked all women and children to return to their houses right away. We all did. My husband had connections in the town. They informed him that the army had left. He thought it was safe to get in touch with us. When we entered the house again, the phone rang. I forgot that the army was outside. I answered it. The army had searched the house and left. I thought they would not return. I did not know that some security men were still outside. They watched and entered houses after the army left. The phone ringtone was loud. I forgot to make it silent.

The security forces were watching us through the windows. They heard the phone ringing. They broke into the house. The phone was still in my hand. With them was a spy who was wearing a face mask. He pointed at me and said, "This house, her husband is working for the Free Army fighters." They knew what my husband was doing. They were looking for him. I canceled the call immediately.

My husband called back.

They became suspicious. I had to answer. I answered, but instead of mentioning my husband's name, I said, "Muhammad, send your mother my way." They were listening and watching me. They said, "Who is this? Is this your husband, Atef?" I said, "No, no, it is my nephew. I swear, sir, it is my nephew." I was hoping my husband would get the message when he heard me saying what I said. I was hoping he would understand the situation. So I ended the call.

But my husband called for the third time.

The spy said, "You are lying. This is not Muhammad. This is Atef." I had to swear by God and lie that it was Muhammad, my nephew. I answered the call and said, "Muhammad, listen to me." He answered, "Muhammad who? Aneesa, I am not Muhammad. I am Atef." The officer heard this. The officer made me put the phone on speaker. He dragged me to the kitchen and left my children in the living room. My husband could not hear the children crying. The officer held the phone and stopped me from ending the call.

Suddenly, we heard loud explosions outside. The screams of people attacking each other next to our house filled the space. The officers took my phone with them. They destroyed what they could from the house and left. We found the phone thrown outside the house after they left. While I was in the kitchen with them, my sister-in-law had entered the house, and the children told her what happened. Then the officers threw her out. She went running to her house. She called Atef and told him what happened. She told him, "They are looking for you. Your family is in danger now."

Atef escaped that day. We moved from our house.

Inspecting Corpses

Shortly after we left, we received news that my brother had been killed. I could not go to his funeral. Around the Adha holiday, my husband called again and said he would pick me and the children up to go see my family. They had moved to another town called al-Qunaitra. He picked us up and dropped us there, where my family was. He was supposed to return to pick us up. We waited for several days before we were informed of his capture at one of the checkpoints. We waited for his release for months. He was not released. We then received news that the Shiites had killed him. Some say the Shiites believe if they kill a Sunni Muslim, they go to heaven. We used to live peacefully with them. Only after the war did we discover that we were living and eating with our enemies. But what happened to them after war? Assad played us against each other. This is how he is winning the war.

My mother-in-law went to find her son's corpse. She inspected many dead men. She flipped their bodies over. She looked for her son. They had thrown the bodies on the ground outside the town. They called mothers to the area to find their sons. Some were headless. Some had been cut into pieces. My mother-in-law could not find her son among them. Some said they might have thrown him in a river. Days passed, and we did not learn anything about him. He just disappeared.

It has been several years since we heard anything about him. He might be alive, who knows? But the truth is, we are convinced he is dead. I moved to live next to my family, and then when their town was bombed, we were left with no choice but to move to Jordan.

Eating Cats in al-Hajar al-Aswad

A neighboring town in Damascus was under terrible conditions. We heard people in al-Hajar al-Aswad had to eat cats to survive. The town was under siege. No one could leave the house. Nothing was delivered to them. They had to eat whatever they found to survive. It was terrible. It is hard to believe. Grass. Tree leaves. Cats. Survival became the one and only goal. We nearly went through the same situation in my town. The bombings would not stop. I moved with my family here right away. We thought in a few months we would return to Syria. I ended up staying. The thought of returning stopped me from finding a way to live here. I started living and looking at things from a different perspective. In the end, we will return if we are meant to.

Sand and Dust

I still remember how I refused to accept the situation here upon our arrival. We are used to being clean and tidy. We had so much clean water. Here, we lived in tents at first. The sand made it impossible to keep our living spaces or the children clean. All efforts to keep things clean were futile. At some point, I found myself wishing a bomb would land by mistake on all of us and we would die instantly.

When we decided to come to Jordan, we did not know what to think of what would later become our life. Sitting in the reception tents upon our arrival. Seeing the sand and the dust. I started crying hysterically. It was not possible to live in such conditions. We survived the camp but at the expense of our health. Our children got sick all the time. Poverty, dirty water—they did not even have the food coupons then. Everything was beyond our financial means.

This is the first year we have felt comfortable here. Thank God, life got better. A caravan changes a refugee's life. We can finally clean it and feel human. We can clean our caravan and wash it. We can look around and feel good. It cannot be compared to a tent. It is true that it is like living in one room, but spacewise, we feel like we have a house. A caravan is a huge upgrade from a tent.

I am optimistic. My story is like that of tens of thousands here. Yes, some have husbands, but their husbands cannot find jobs. Some are depressed. Some make their wives' lives harder. I am happier this way. No misery or daily drama. Just my children to focus on.

"Dad Is Up in Heaven"

When my husband left to fight, I was already pregnant with my youngest. My past four deliveries were difficult. They were cesarean. I had a son and three daughters. I decided not to check the sex of my fifth baby, in hopes that God would surprise us with a brother to my son. When my husband left, I was six months' pregnant. He did not know if it was a boy or a girl. He never knew. I delivered a baby boy.

He has never seen his dad. If you ask him, "Where is Baba?"

He points to the sky and answers, "Dad is up in heaven."

I will not get married again. The majority of Syrian widows never remarry when their husbands die. My children are my life.

CHAPTER 4

Memories and Tribulations

Memories Left Behind
Amal

I often daydream about returning.

I daydream about going back and seeing my friends at the cafeteria. We always had breakfast there together. We gossiped together. We laughed over bad jokes. We were happy.

I wish I could share my feelings with them now.

I miss my life in Syria. I miss having friends I trust. I miss being happy. I wonder sometimes if we were truly ever happy . . . if we *really* enjoyed our lives. Every day I forget something from my past, and I get scared. I am scared that one day I will no longer recall good memories of my past and I will convince myself that life was never good. I do not want to get used to living here. Life would be meaningless.

I would give up everything for a conversation with any of my friends. I wish to relive one of those days.

I often think of my friends and wonder where they are. I wonder, *Were we ever friends? Do they still think of me? Do they know I am a refugee? Do they know what life is like here?* Maybe they read about us in the newspapers. Maybe they hear about us in the news. Maybe they've been wishing me luck.

Maybe they think I was killed.

Whatever they think, I just hope they remember me. I hope they remember the happy girl I once was. I had so many plans. I was ready to fight the world.

Now I am starting to doubt my own recollection of my life. I hope they never let my memory die. I hope they are all fine and safe.

Treasure Box
Nuha

I left behind a treasure in Syria. I buried it in a secret location. Let me tell you, it took me over two years to finally know it was still there.

When the soldiers entered our village, we were advised to take our children and run right away. It was the middle of a cold night, and despite knowing that this moment would eventually come, I discovered I had not prepared for it. I collected my children and ran.

Then I remembered the treasure.

It was not gold or money. It was our family photos. All in a big box under our bed. I asked for a minute and ran like a madwoman to the house. I opened the door, ran to our bedroom, and grabbed the box like I would hold my child. Mesmerized, I stood there for a minute that felt like eternity. I could not take it with me. I ran to the big wooden table in our living room. I do not know why I chose that place to hide the box. I thought the soldiers would go directly to our bedroom and destroy it instead of looking under a wooden table in the living room. No one would expect to find something of value under a wooden table.

I stood there. I held the box close to me. I wept. I knew I had no time: I heard people screaming, asking me to hurry before a bomb falls on our heads. I hid the box under the wooden table. I said a quick prayer. Quietly, I apologized to the photos. I felt I was betraying the memories.

These were not just photos. They were the record of my entire life. I inherited some from my parents. All the memories of my children and my marriage and friendships were guarded in these photos.

I was saying my farewell to them in the midst of war. Leaving them behind was one of the hardest things this war made me do.

It took a long time, but I finally made sure they were still there. After arriving at the camp, I sent messages with anyone from our area who returned to Syria. Anyone who dared visit the village after its destruction. I asked them to visit our house and check under the wooden table. After several attempts, a neighbor found the box.

I have not seen the photos yet because he is unable to transport the box to the camp. However, you have no idea how happy I became when I received the news of its rescue. The rooms in our house had been leveled to the ground, but thank God, the box survived under the table. The news of its survival pumped a new life through me.

I know you see tears in my eyes now. Please forgive me, I cannot help it. Our photos became the only proof and reminder that we once had a wonderful life. This box is as dear to me as my life. I am so grateful it is safe. I need these photos to remember who I once was.

A Haunting Past
Wahijaa

I am not going to complain about money or food. That's not an issue. We survive on vegetables and beans. As we say in Arabic, "Hunger alone will not kill you." I am not going to talk about war and death. Everybody in the camp lost someone or is waiting for the news of the death of a dear one. We are equal in this regard. My husband was shot in Syria. He died instantly. That is okay. God gives. God takes. No problem. I am doing my best for my children. God willing, I will be rewarded in the hereafter.

I came here to talk to you in hopes that you will help me. I am a good woman in general. Selfless and caring. But after I was widowed several years ago and we came to the camp, I became an abusive mother. I accuse my daughters of things they have not done. I shame them in public. Especially my nine-year-old daughter, Warda. I am worried people will say I could not bring her up properly by myself. I overwork her with the housework.

I berate her if I happen to see her not well dressed or clean. I am very, very nervous.

I cannot stand to see any girl doing better than my daughter. I love Warda and her two sisters, Noora and Nadia. I scream at Warda in front of her sisters. I spank her. I thought this would teach her sisters to be better daughters. I tell her that the neighbor's daughter is more beautiful than her. That the neighbor's daughter is better than her. I hoped this would make Warda jealous. I hoped this would make her want to become the best girl. I want Warda to look good and be tidy. She wants to change her clothes more than once a day. Other girls here change their clothes once every three or four days while managing to remain clean. They look great. She plays with dirt, and her clothes become dirty. She should be more careful.

Warda is not smart. Maybe she is lazy. She does not wash dishes or clean the caravan as good as her younger sisters. I have to make her clean and help. I worry this is an indication of the woman she will become in the future. I worry her in-laws will say I failed in teaching her good manners. Good skills. I failed in teaching her to be clean and tidy all the time. The in-laws will blame me. She cries and asks me to stop picking on her. I cannot stop.

This would never happen in Syria. There I was in control of my household. Here you cannot control everything. This happens every day. I feel so sorry because I cannot contain my rage. I find myself belittling and spanking her often. I had an abusive mother. I still cannot get over what she said and did to me. I cannot forgive her. But I tell myself that this is different. The circumstances are different now.

I am not in Syria. I am in a camp. The caravans are so close to each other. People hear and see everything. There is no privacy. People criticize each other all the time. I wake up every day and promise myself to try other ways with my daughter. But I fail. I am depressed. I am very exhausted. Her father is dead. She says she wishes he was around so she could complain to him. So she could put her head on his shoulder and cry. She has no one in the camp but me and her siblings. I love her. I admit to having a serious issue to address in disciplining my children. I am unable to change how I act or what I say.

No matter how hard I try not to say an offensive word, I find myself saying it to her. The way I was raised messed with my mind. I do not understand why I say what I say. My lips just say things I do not mean. I repeat some of what I heard from my mother as a child and a teenager when she does not listen to me. I despise that. But I cannot change that. It is like I know how much it hurt me, yet I am unable to stop hurting the ones I love and care about.

I forbid Warda from leaving the caravan except to go to an educational club. She listens to me. I am under so much pressure. My son is a boy. It does not matter what he does. No one criticizes boys. I need help to deal with my anger issues. I am torn between what I want to do and what I end up doing. I want to be a better mother. I do not want to be my mother. I do not want my daughter to hate me. I do not want to hurt her. I am hurt and stuck.

A Necessary Lie

My second daughter, Noora, just had an eye operation. Four months ago she was playing with a knife. She fell and the knife cut her eye. Noora was in so much pain. Al-Awan medical NGO here helped her. The NGO facilitates and sponsors her treatment in a hospital outside the camp now. She is still able to see with her injured eye. It is looking more normal with every passing day. The doctors assured me that with time she will get better.

I dealt with becoming a widow at an early age. I am dealing with being a refugee woman with children alone here. I am overcoming the hurdles one by one. When my daughter fell, I felt like I am never given a break. I worry about her all the time. Whenever we return from the hospital, people inquire about her health. I tell them the doctors said she is doing great. I say she does not need an eye operation or further treatment. I lie to them. I cannot share the truth about her medical condition with others. People gossip and exaggerate. They may be saying she lost sight in that eye. Rumors like this complicate her marriage chances in the future. Like any other mother, I want the best for my daughters. I am working on becoming a mother. I would not hesitate to do anything to protect them. Social stigma and shaming are inescapable in the Arab world in general and in the camp in particular, especially if you are a female.

So many of us here are widowed mothers dealing with mounting challenges. I want to protect my children. I am aware I need to address several issues in my life. Some are related to my past. Others are related to this community and living conditions. No one is perfect. If I am able to address what challenges and pains me and my family, it will be easier to manage life. The main problems are within people themselves, not others. I am able to limit my interactions with the people I do not feel comfortable around. I am able to help my children with schoolwork. But I am unable to help myself deal with sudden social and emotional challenges. I will speak to the Women's Center soon. They have experts who can guide me through this difficult time. I want to overcome this now.

I hope I will become better equipped to manage life under stress. I hope life will get better for everyone. I am thankful for the support of Jordanians here. They have done all they can to help us. We are one extended family. It is just that no one should look for an ideal life at a camp. Every caravan is wounded. Every family went through tragic events. Happiness is not meant to be complete no matter what you do. I am content with what I have. I am confident everything will be better.

An Escape Plan
Sulafa

I left Syria in late 2013. My husband died under shelling. I left with my daughter and son. When I arrived, I lived with the sons of my husband's ex-wife. I kept asking for a caravan. After five months, someone donated money to buy new caravans. I was on the waiting list. Finally, we had a caravan for ourselves.

My son was born in 1994. He got bored here. He complained a lot about the camp. He informed me of his decision to return to Syria. This means he is going to die. We cannot return now. My husband is

gone. I love him so much. I feel his pain. Day and night, I kept thinking of ways to stop him. I talked to him for weeks. I begged him not
to go. He could not stay. He said he is dying slowly here. He said he
cannot watch war from afar when he is able to fight back against
Assad. He could not get over the death of his father and other relatives in Syria. He could not waste his time here doing nothing when
he is able to be of use in Syria. He said he could at least go die to serve
his country.

I thought to myself, *If my son gets married, he might change his
mind.* I got him married a year ago. He lives with his wife. I insisted
that as newlyweds, they should have the caravan room for themselves.
My daughter and I slept in a tent adjoining the caravan for some time.
We saved some money. We bought a caravan from a family. My son is
a young man. His wife is pregnant. He still could not find a job here.
Syrians are not going to die of hunger—we have food—but there are
no jobs. He is jobless. His wife will have a baby soon.

I have faith life might get better one day. I just want to see him
stay here. It pains me to see him like this. I love him so much. He is
my baby. I understand how he feels. But I am not a magician. I cannot change the way things are. I am living in constant fear that I will
lose him one day, that I will wake up in the morning to find him
gone. I cry whenever I talk about him. My children are my life.

He said once that when his wife delivers the baby, he will leave
for Syria. It is a tough position to be in. He leaves and looks for a job
every day. He is gifted and can do a lot. His attempts to find a job
failed. He escaped secretly at night a couple of times to a surrounding town. He would come home at night very exhausted and hungry.
He lost weight and did not talk much. I could not see him like that.
Some of his friends escaped for a day or two to work there. There are
opportunities outside the camp. I worried the camp guards would
catch him one day. If they catch him sneaking outside the camp to
work, they threatened they will hurl him back to Syria. I lived in fear
until he returned. I would hug him and make him promise me not to
go again. He no longer leaves.

I trust God will not forget us. I do not know what to do. I just
pray for a change. We were fine in Syria. Now we are suffocating

from all sides. Lack of opportunity is the biggest hurdle. If only the men could work. That is all I ask for. He looked for any possible job to support his family. He was able to land a part-time job. He worked as a janitor for a few months. Then it was someone else's turn to get the job. He made thirty dinars.

Sometimes you have to leave the camp to see a doctor, but the permit to leave takes a long time. Clinics here are good, but if you need a specialist, you have to go outside. I wish they would give more permits to women. I am a widow. What security threat do I pose? I remind myself that now we sleep peacefully far from bombing. I am grateful for that.

The Mosque Instead of the School

My daughter, Rawan, is fifteen years old. She went to school here for a few months. Then she stopped. Some bad guys followed her to the caravan many times. She cried. Rawan did so well at school. But it is not a good place for her now. We did not report the bad guys because we did not want them to be hurled back to Syria. I told them to stop coming around. But they do not listen. Now she goes to the mosque to study with her friends. I teach her also at home.

I am from Hama. I passed high school and then got married at the age of twenty. But life here is different, so I do not know when Rawan will get married. We used to hear terrible stories about al-Zaatari Camp when we were in Syria. Stories of possible rape and violence. My in-laws were angry that we came here. But when we came, we found that it is safe. The only problem is that we only have electricity from 7:00 p.m. to 5:00 a.m., and that was only during the holy month of Ramadan. For the seven months prior to that we did not have electricity. If only we could have electricity for longer hours. If only our young men could have jobs. I pray war ends and we return to Syria soon.

Saving a Pregnancy
Wafa

I just discovered I am pregnant again. This is my second month. My husband and I have five beautiful children.

Given the situation at the camp, we decided we do not want more children. I do not use the pill. I got pregnant again. I do not know what to do. My husband said I need to end this pregnancy today if I want to return home. He wants an abortion.

I will not have an abortion.

This might not be the last time I get pregnant. I do not know what to do. I do not know how to feel about my body right now. I feel my husband hates me. I keep getting pregnant. I do not want more children. I want to take care of those I already have. This pregnancy may cost me my marriage and children. My husband cannot provide for six children, himself, and a wife. We do not have enough food for the children. We cannot cover basic needs like diapers and milk for the little ones.

I came to the camp with my husband and children. All my family and relatives are in Syria. My children need me right now. I need to return to them. A woman encouraged me to seek help from the Family Protection Center. I am on my way. They have to find me a solution. I do not want to be divorced and kept away from my children. I cannot take any more abuse. My baby has been crying for hours. She is so hungry. I have not fed her since the morning. I have milk powder but no clean water.

A Breath of Dust
Umm Manal

Upon arriving at the camp in 2012 we quickly learned that the scattered tents across the Jordanian desert are our home now. At least until the war is over.

People were arriving in great numbers day and night. It was chaotic. We focused on getting settled in one of the tents in a good district. As soon as tents were starting to be replaced with caravans, we were among the first to demand moving into a caravan. Tents could protect us from neither cold nor hot weather conditions.

The move into a caravan was a major change. I have never imagined I would wish for a caravan to become my home. Fleeing war and bombs in Syria safely with our children was the most important thing for us. When we were running in the middle of the night and looking for a car to transport us to Jordan, it did not cross our minds that we would soon be living in tents in the desert and wishing to be granted a caravan. I could not help but compare our beautiful home and the green garden surrounding it in Syria to the tent we were told is all we have now. I would wake up in the middle of the night thinking we were at our home. I would dream of going places and driving my car, only to wake up in the morning to face the grim reality at the camp. No cars. No house. No friends. No work. No green. No life.

Sand was everywhere.

Sand was in our eyes. Sand was in our clothes. Sand became a layer on our faces. No matter how many times I cleaned the caravan, sand found its way back everywhere. It is still in our water, in our eyes, in our lungs. Everywhere. But this is no longer important. We gave up on hating sand. For now, the desert is home.

One day, I woke up early and started preparing something for us to eat. My husband left to go to the al-Zaatari market to get us some bread and tomatoes. He returned, we all ate, and then he left to talk to a guy who promised to help him find a job. I got bored at home, so I decided to visit my neighbor, Alia. I took my daughter with me and left.

I arrived at Alia's tent. I heard her inside talking to someone. But she would not welcome me to come in. I knew she was there.

I knew something was not right.

I called to her a couple times. Alia finally asked me to come in, and I did. Alia's daughter, Farah, was sitting next to her. Farah was crying. I gave my daughter to Farah and asked her to go walk outside near the caravan to improve her mood while I talked to her mother. After she left, I asked Alia what was going on.

Alia hesitated, but then she said, "Farah is getting married next week." I did not know how to respond. Marriage is a happy occasion, but since they were crying, I figured it must be a bad one. But I was a fool. I had forgotten that Farah was not old enough to get married. As soon as I remembered, I said, "Oh no, she is young."

It was no secret that early marriages are failures.

It is hard for young grooms and the brides to understand what marriage is about. When you marry a man, you also marry his family. I was eighteen when I got married. It was not easy for me to manage my life with my in-laws in Syria. Look at me: I have one daughter, and we can hardly take care of her. It is very hard being a refugee, and it is a million times harder being a female refugee.

As a female refugee, you need your father and brothers to protect you here. If you do not have male relatives, you have to protect yourself. Some families see marriage as a way to protect their girls and provide them with a better life in the camp. But while marriage sometimes saves girls from one hell, it throws them into a new hell. You know, when girls have babies at an early age, it is like a baby carrying a baby.

I once saw a girl trying on a wedding dress here in the market. There are a few stores, and they are popular. The dress was long and white. The girl was tiny. She was so excited. She looked very beautiful. I saw her cherish that moment of joy. I imagined her a bride and then, of course, after a few months, pregnant. But I could not help but imagine her giving birth. I had a terrible birth experience. I almost died giving birth to my daughter. After my marriage at the age of eighteen, I realized that early marriages like mine are tough. You need to have a good experience in life before you become a wife or a mother. I no longer approve of early marriages. Especially when you are not in your home. Not in a camp, for heaven's sake.

I looked again at the girl. She was too young to carry a human being inside her. She seemed like a baby herself, so how could she deliver a baby? I did not say a word to her mother. I prayed for her and her daughter.

Every time I hear a story like this, I think of my daughter and worry about her. We worry that something might happen to us, and she will be fragile and alone here. I try to make good relationships with people here so that if something happens to us, they will take care of her. We are healthy, but in this world you never know what might happen to you tomorrow. I sometimes worry a bomb will hit our caravan and we will all die. I wake up in the middle of the night breathless, thinking someone has shot her or her father. Then I see them sleeping next to me, and I thank God dearly for that.

All I want nowadays is safety and peace. I hope Syria will be liberated from ISIS and Assad and we can return to rebuild it again. I wish for my daughter to return and go to school and university. I want her to have a job and a good life. I hope by the time she is fifteen or sixteen, Syria will be back. I hope this war will not last for more than ten years. It must end one day. But I also worry about the time my daughter spends here. It is over for us. We are surviving this, but for our daughter, this is not okay. She will not have a good life here, and she will not get a good education. There are schools here, but I am not sure they are good. It is like killing time, pretending to go to school. I hear that more and more girls drop out of school every day. The schools might get better with time—like everything else, we hope—but still, it is not what you would hope for the human dearest to your heart, your son or daughter.

I often find myself talking to God. At night, when everyone goes to sleep, or when everyone says they are going to sleep, I read the Quran. I read it because it says justice will prevail and God will not let us down. It has been hard to explain to children at the camp why God would allow such things to happen to innocent people like us or innocent children like them.

A child saw his friend die in front of their yard after it was bombed by the regime. He has been struggling with nightmares since arriving at the camp. He keeps asking adults why God would let his friend die like this. We told him we do not have answers for all questions. We said God for sure must have a great plan and a good ending for this sad story. But I myself wonder sometimes, *Why do we have to pay this price?* I understand that men might die in war. I understand that women might die as well. But children? How could we watch them die like this?

For what good would an eight-year-old lose his arms and legs in the name of war? I read God's words. They provide me with so much peace and faith. But it is not transferable. I am unable to give some of that to children. They cannot understand the Quran the way adults do. Nothing seems to make us feel better. We keep telling them it is God's wisdom, which no one should question.

But children say this is no wisdom.

We tell them to never repeat such words. I am afraid they are troubled. I know so many little children are in heaven now. But children do not understand heaven and hell well. They do not believe children have to die this way to be in heaven. I ask God to strengthen my faith, to end this war as soon as possible. I do not want to lose my faith.

The Brother-in-Law Moves In

Did you hear that sound? It was my brother-in-law. He has just entered the caravan and left quickly. He came over a year ago from Syria by himself. He had no place to go, so my husband invited him to live with us in our caravan. As you see, the caravan is so small, and with another man living with us, I am suffocating.

I have zero privacy. I am always stressed. I cannot even take my scarf off during the day because he is around most of the time. I told my husband that this is an impossible situation. He insists he has no solution and his brother has nowhere else to go. I miss the days when I had the caravan all to myself and my husband and daughter. I could have guests, but now my female friends hesitate to visit me because there is no privacy in our small caravan. I cannot even lie in this room during the day because he might enter the caravan at any minute. It is like living as a traveler around the clock.

I wish the camp administration could help us with this. He is by himself, so they will not give him a caravan. But this should not be my problem: I already have a hundred problems to worry about. I do not mean to sound mean, but I am so tired of this. I even started fighting with my husband because of this pressure in our life. With a baby and a brother-in-law to worry about, I feel like I cannot manage this life like I should. I wish to live a normal married life, but I cannot. I told my husband we cannot have a second child under these conditions, but I know we will. He wants more children. It is a mistake to do so now.

Well, I am so sorry I burdened you with my story, but I do not know what to do. You will be happy when you have children outside the camp. It is a beautiful blessing from God but not inside the camp. Everything is beautiful from God, but having children here makes life harder on us and on the children. Why would you bring pure, innocent souls to life, only to be tortured in here? I will certainly have more children if we return to Syria. But here, it is like torturing the ones you love most.

Life is not only eating and breathing. Look around you: you see we have what we need, thank God. I just want peace of mind and a normal life. I miss my husband. I miss talking and joking with him and staying up late remembering the good old days in Syria. Since his brother joined us here, it has been difficult to have a private time with him. Either he is with his brother or his brother is with us.

"Some Say It's Black Magic"
Umm Muhammad

I have been at the camp since early 2013. I am here with my daughter and husband. Because of his injury, he cannot work. My daughter is in her forties; she never got married. We are given sixty Jordanian dinars a month, which is not enough. We had a piece of land in Syria, which we sold before coming here.

I do not leave our caravan. I have four daughters and two sons in Syria. They cry, for we are apart. They beg me to go there. I need to go see my children, but I do not want to return. I have a young daughter in Syria who is also unmarried. She calls us and begs me to go back. They need me with them. But we cannot pay for the return expenses. I tell them I cannot do anything about it.

My son lived here with us for two and a half months when we first arrived. Then he returned to Syria and joined the Free Syrian Army. His wife, whom he left here, was pregnant and had a baby girl. She got sick, and he kept calling and asking if I would return with his wife and daughter. Or if I would send them to him. We asked his wife if she wanted to go, and she said yes. She took her daughter and went to him. Since then they have been asking me to return.

I cannot walk like I used to. I do not go anywhere. I sit with my husband all day long. Doing nothing, hoping something will change. Last winter was so hard. We had no source of warmth. We bundled up and huddled in the corner of the caravan. To buy gas we needed three dinars every couple of days. We could not afford it. My daughter helped pay for that. She does not have a job, and she does not make money. But she managed to help us. She is by herself with her five children. It is safe here. My other daughter has eight daughters. Four got married, and four haven't yet. They do not go to school here. They tried to enroll in school, but they missed the first academic semester. We lost Syria, there is no point in making a big deal of losing the opportunity of education in a camp.

One of my granddaughters, Buthania, got sick after she was engaged. The afternoon of her engagement, she went to the market with her fiancé. That evening, after they returned, she came to see me. She said she was not feeling well. I read some verses from the Quran on her and prayed for her that night. Then she went to her mother's caravan. Later that day, her sister screamed and called us to go see her. We found Buthania in her mother's lap. She was so sick. Concerned neighbors rushed to their caravan. They took her to the doctor right away. No one knows what's wrong with her. She kept fainting and losing consciousness.

Some say it's black magic. The doctors could not figure it out.

Buthania stayed with her husband here for some time after they got married in Syria. Whenever she is upset, she loses consciousness and faints. Their marriage is documented only in Syria. Her husband left the camp to fight with the Free Syrian Army. She followed him afterward. Her mother did not want her to leave the camp by herself. The Free Syrian Army sent someone to escort her. She is in Syria now. She does not have children yet. Her husband is fighting in another town.

Buthania has been through tragic times. She does not have children. There is no reason for her to stay in this relationship. I believe it is better for her to return to the camp. She said she returned to be with her husband, but she does not see him anymore. Her husband keeps calling us. He says he loves her and he wants her. The town where she lives is al-Sanamein. It is controlled by Assad's forces now. He is fighting in another town. They cannot be together.

Therefore, there is no reason for her to stay by herself in that town. She will need someone to take care of her when she gets sick. We want to take care of her. She is our daughter. She did not get married to be by herself with her mother-in-law. We want to help her return to us. We do not have the money to secure a ride for her back here, but we are looking for a solution. I will borrow money and send it to her to secure a ride back. She wants to return. It takes two weeks on al-Ruwaished desert road to get here. We need someone to accompany her, so we have to pay travel expenses for two.

Buthania's complicated experience and disappointing marriage made me certain that my other daughters should not get married anytime soon. Marriage here creates problems more than it solves. If we return to our homes and towns, then the situation will change. Otherwise, we cannot keep adding drama to the already messy situation here. Our daughters are happier with us than with someone they would call a husband on paper.

CHAPTER 5

Saving the Children

Too Young to Understand
Saja

My daughter came home from school one day and said she no longer wants to go. I asked her why, and she said she just does not like school here. I did not know what was happening and worried that Noora was being bullied. I heard stories about schools being unsafe, but I had no way of knowing the truth. Other girls were also dropping out of school, too. So we allowed her to stay home.

It was a mistake.

After a few months of staying at home, Noora missed her friends. She wanted to return to school. We did not know what to do. She could not return. She got sad and refused to talk to us.

It pained me to see her cry. I, too, cried next to her bed. She just did not know it.

I cannot sleep at night. I am worried about her. I hear scary stories every day. I fear we lost the bond we had back in Syria. We were really close, and we spent a lot of time talking every day. I feel I do not know her well anymore.

The camp changed her.

She has become stubborn, and she sometimes says things she does not mean. I am worried one day I will wake up and find out she has left our caravan.

My husband was already sick when we were in Syria. He became depressed here. Losing his job crushed him. He keeps saying he has turned into a useless man. He says he wishes to die every day. I pray war ends and we return home. We need to return home.

We argue every day. I argue with my husband and kids all the time. I have been married for twenty years, and we rarely had a serious argument. We used to work things out. Now, it is strange what has happened to us. He changed; he is another man. The children changed. I changed. Everything changed.

I am a mother. It's natural that I empathize with everyone. I am trying to help my family. I do not want to see them give up. I do not want the war and the camp to break my family. I do not know what to do next, but I know we need to listen to each other and understand that we are not at home. We cannot afford the life we had in Syria. Children cannot understand; they are very young. They think we intentionally refuse to get them what they want. I tried to explain it to them many times, but it is beyond their comprehension. I cannot control life in the camp. I blame no one, except war. War is a catastrophe. Even if we return home, we will not be the same people. I can see how war changed us all.

Once some things are lost, you cannot restore them.

You won't believe how I used to be. I looked better than this. I dressed better. And I enjoyed the little things. I loved to dress up and go shopping at the mall with friends. I loved to sleep in on weekends after a busy week at work.

Now I miss buying groceries and drinking coffee with my daughter afterward. I miss seeing the family sit together at home.

I miss breathing with ease.

Children of the Camp
Rania

I lost my husband to war in Syria. I lost my children to the camp.

My five children were well behaved in Syria. Something changed since we arrived here two years ago. The eldest two boys go outside the caravan. When they come back, they say the insults and cuss words they hear. They do not listen to me no matter how many times I tell them not to repeat at home what they hear in the streets of the camp. This upsets me very much. I enrolled them in school. The school dismissed them because of their behavior. I pleaded with the teachers to take them back, to give them a second chance. They were kind to give them another chance.

In less than a week, they were dismissed.

They are so young—just ten and fourteen—but they quickly absorbed the madness in here. They throw things at me when they are angry. They blame me for bringing them here. They want better food, clothes, and shoes. I have none to give them.

I have no family here except for my children. I do not want to lose them.

I wait until the beginning of each month. We get twenty Jordanian dinars per family member. The camp administration gives us the money in a debit card, but you can only use it in specific shops, such as the mall. Everything is expensive there. I sell our debit card to others for cash, far less than its value. Although I get less money, with cash I am free to shop anywhere at the camp. I get cheaper stuff this way.

The majority of the people I know sell their debit cards. We use cash to pay some debt and get by as well.

It is difficult to support five children by myself in a camp. My oldest daughter is a wonderful girl. She goes to school, and her teachers love her. She helps me around the house. She does not cause trouble. My problem is with her two brothers. I fear they will start causing big trouble in the camp. I worry they might get arrested one day.

I have nobody here. I am losing my children to the camp.

You know, I tried everything with them. I talked nicely to them. I disciplined them. I slapped them. Nothing I tried worked. One day I told my son, "If you keep talking like this to your sister and me, if you keep causing trouble in the streets of the camp, if you continue to misbehave, I will report you to the camp administration. Do you want to be sent back to Syria?" He said he would go himself and tell the administration that he wants to go back to Syria. I was shocked at how desperate they've become. He said he would also tell them that

I cursed the Jordanian government and monarch so they would throw me in prison. Can you believe my son said that to me?

I did not know what to do. That evening, he left the caravan and did not return until midnight. I started crying. I had no idea what he was doing.

I wish his dad was around.

I am disappointed in what my sons have become. The camp ruined their childhood. They refuse to go to school, they do not speak kindly to others, and they spend their time with the wrong crowd. I no longer know how to deal with them. There is nothing I can do to correct their behavior.

Their father was a brave man. Everyone spoke of his courage. He stood against Assad's tyranny. He was among the first men to fight and fall as a *shaheed* [martyr] during the revolution. He gave his life for Syria and for his children.

I tell myself, at least he is now in a better place.

We had to leave right away when we learned that he was killed. My in-laws took themselves to Amman. They had some money, so they could afford it. We had nothing. We ended up in the camp.

This war is a tragedy. There are no winners. What has been taken from Syria and Syrians cannot be returned. These children have lost everything.

How can I raise five children with twenty dinars a month each?

I asked for more financial support from the camp administration. I heard that several Arab and Muslim organizations give out extra money for the children of martyrs. We never received anything. I inquired. We were told we were outside the camp when the families of martyrs received the donations. But no one knows when to expect such donations. When they become available, they get distributed. If you are not present in the camp, you are not included.

It happened twice thus far. I was visiting with my in-laws in Amman each time.

My in-laws are another story. They want to see the children once a month. They do not support them. They only ask to see them. They blame me for failing to bring them up. They do not feel for a mother with five children in the camp. They do not even try to understand. They never suggested that we leave the camp and live with them.

How can they not care for the children of their own son? Their father is gone. My family is far away in Syria.

I am the mother of my children. I will keep doing my best despite this. I will not give up. I promised their father to never give up. I am feeling more and more like an outsider. My in-laws are planning for my daughter to get married in a few years. When I objected, they said they are her family. They claimed I was an outsider. They said she is *their* daughter. She carries their family name.

They broke my heart. I will not let them break me.

Every time we meet they remind me she is to be married soon. They do not want her to marry someone from the camp. They believe they know what's best for her. I will have to face this soon. I hate to think of that, but I am not sure what to do.

The children are growing up quickly. It is getting harder to take care of them. I do not know how to do it anymore. One day I may have to take them and return to Syria. It can't be worse than this. I have reached the last of my nerves.

I know you are listening to me, but let me tell you the truth. You cannot help me in any way. I have to help myself.

I worked in several stores here. I worked in a salon, then in a bridal gown shop, then in international organizations. You usually work for one month, then they ask you to leave because they are not making enough money. Disappointments and rejections follow one another until your spirit dies off. I still look for a job every day. I am willing to work and learn any profession. But, tell me, what on earth can I do that I haven't done? Tell me, how on earth am I supposed manage this?

I am worried that, sooner rather than later, my pent-up anger will overwhelm me suddenly and perhaps even kill me. I cannot even call myself an insider with my own children. I cannot look in my daughter's eyes anymore. With each day that passes, she gets closer to leaving us. She is the only good thing in my life, and I am going to lose her soon. I already lost her brothers and father. My only wish now is that they will not get us in big trouble with the camp families or administration.

Did their father think this would happen? I would not wish for him to know what we have become. But he knew his family well. He knew they would not care about us. When he disappeared, we were still in our town. My in-laws lived close to our house, but they never checked on us. I used to be a housewife; I never went farther than a few houses from our house. When we were trapped in town by the war and my husband never returned, I had to leave the house daily at three o'clock in the morning to get food and other things for the children. I had to work outside the house until late at night to get enough to survive.

Why did he leave us to no one? How could he suddenly go like this?

Gracious Heart
Sawsan

My baby, Karim, was born with Down syndrome. I found out only after giving birth to him in a hospital outside the camp.

The doctor said I should have been informed about my child's medical situation while I was pregnant. No one told me anything at the camp. The doctor asked me to share the news with my husband.

And then he left.

It was one of the hardest moments in my life. We tried seven years to have a child. Why did this happen? And how would I sit there and watch my husband break as I break such news to him?

I love Karim. I welcome God's wisdom and choice with a gracious heart. I just wish the doctors had told me before his birth. We had months. Having to deal with this news right after delivery was heartbreaking. It has been so hard to get any medical care for Karim in the camp. His temperature goes up all the time. I watch helplessly as he boils like hot water in front of me. I ask for help. Do you know what I hear?

Your baby is not normal. Relax.

This is the life you should expect for him.

They cannot feel my pain—or maybe they do, but they do not understand. Maybe they are not equipped to treat babies with special needs like Karim. He would die if we did not take him to a private hospital outside the camp. We cannot afford the high expenses anymore.

My baby struggles here. I wish I could give him a better life.

Any time he needs medical attention, I want to carry him and run to a hospital, a medical center, anywhere. But we live in the camp. We're stuck. There aren't many cases like that of my baby's here. The hospitals cannot do much for babies with Down syndrome. Employees are overworked. They have to provide services to too many refugees every day. They are understaffed. But what can we do? Where else do we go?

I hate feeling I am seeking charity. I do not need sympathy—I need help. He is just a baby. He deserves to live. He deserves to receive medical attention like normal babies because he *is* normal. He is an unlucky baby in the wrong place. I often wonder what kind of life awaits him. We have to remain optimistic no matter what happens.

Sometimes I regret fleeing here. It's not the country but my children. There is no worse feeling than a mother who cannot help her own children.

I know I could have died in Syria. Now I have to watch my baby suffer like this. People tell me I should be thankful because otherwise we would be dead in Syria. I should be grateful to be alive, they say.

But what is left of life when it is reduced to painful breathing? To thought of death?

Child Soldiers
Rida

The living conditions in the camp cause a lot of stress in our life. Life is more complex with a sick husband and several sons. All jobless. If they were children, it would be easier to promise or convince them that life might get better. But they are adults. They know life here is tough. They know life is unlikely to get better.

Like other mothers in the world, I have been through difficult times to protect my children. They do not want to stay in the camp. They want to return to Syria. I hope they listen to me and realize that we must stay here for the time being. My oldest son is twenty-two. He wants to return to our town. I tried everything to stop him from returning. I suggested that he get married to one of the girls here to give him a reason to stay. But he asked, "And how am I going to provide for a wife when I cannot provide for myself? When I have nothing to offer her?" I did not know what to say. I kept silent. I usually do not respond to his questions because that would only result in a heated discussion. He sits at the threshold of the caravan throughout the day. His youth is wasted. He tried to find a job in the market, but there are thousands of young men like him looking for a job every day. The majority of them are turned down. There are more people than jobs. He wanted to escape from the camp to work in one of the surrounding towns at night, but I begged him not to. I worry for his safety.

I have two other sons as well. The middle son has become very moody here. He loses his temper quickly. We argue every day. I keep silent for a couple of days, but then I lose my temper, too, and start screaming at him. My neighbor runs to our caravan and asks me what is wrong when she hears us screaming. It is difficult to have three sons and a husband sitting in the caravan 24/7. Depressed, jobless, and hopeless. It kills them that there is no way out. It kills me to see them die slowly. Especially their father. He is old and sad.

Some guys leave the caravans at night to hang out together to relieve some of the stress. I do not let my sons leave the caravan at night. I worry about them. I do not know who these guys are or where they go at night and what they do. I cry and beg them every night not to go. They sympathize with me and stay at the caravan with broken hearts.

My blood pressure is high. Sometimes I feel like I am going to die. I take medication, sometimes one pill, sometimes two. The situation is getting worse every day. Their father sometimes loses it and tells them to return to Syria. They are the only ones I have left. I left Syria to protect them from war. I do not want to lose them. I do not want them to go fight and die there. For now, I just want them to be here with me. Safe and alive.

M y youngest son is sixteen, and he leaves secretly to work outside the camp. He says, "I am only sixteen, Mum, under the legal age to be returned to Syria if caught sneaking from the camp." So he works at night. He is paying the highest price in the family for being away from home. Every time he leaves, he puts himself in dangerous situations. This breaks my heart. But he says, "I cannot see my family struggle and do nothing. I cannot sit and watch when I am able to do something to help."

He does not make much money. He helps farmers pick fruit, and they give him a few dinars. He did not work when we were in Syria. If only you could see him when he returns from work. Forgive my tears. I am a mother. It tortures me to see my youngest son return in the early hours of the morning like this. Hungry. Exhausted. Thirsty. Scared. I count the minutes for his return. Every time he leaves, I sit and wait for him. I cry. I pray he will return safely without being caught or harmed. There is nothing that I can do to help him. My plea is that of a mother to God, he sees it all, he knows it all. *Inshallah*, everything will get better.

I wish I could do more for him and his brothers. If they catch a refugee working outside the camp without a permit, like my son, and he is over eighteen, they hurl him to Syria. Death awaits the majority of those who return. We hear terrifying stories. They return to bullets, torture, and death. It would help our sons if the camp administration and NGOs would create more opportunities for work. And if they can come up with more flexible plans to help young men work outside the camp. These young men cannot endure what feels like being stuck in an impossible situation like this in the desert.

Children Trying to Commit Suicide

We heard of several young girls and guys trying to commit suicide in various districts. We entered our neighbor's caravan a few weeks ago and found their daughter trying to hang herself. The rope was around her neck. Her mother is scared for her daughter. She no longer trusts her alone: she accompanies her all the time. Before this attempt, the girl had tried to kill herself by overdosing on pills. She is sixteen years old. It was a miracle that she survived.

Everyone tried to convince her not to do it a third time. They told her, "You say if you die, you might rest, but what about your miserable mother? Your brothers and father? What will happen to them? What will people say about them?" They tried to tell her she would go to hell because you cannot take your own life. You are entrusted with your soul by God, so you cannot betray this trust and kill yourself. But the problem is that sometimes she understands and agrees, and other times she is hard to reason with. She is very beautiful. Many men asked for her hand, but she is still young to get married.

Life here is hard. People are scared. If you do anything the camp administration does not permit, they might hurl you back to Syria. We would love to go back and live in our country; this is not the life anyone wants for their children. But if we return now, we return to torture cells and graveyards.

Dignified Death

I was scared for my daughter's safety, so I came here. Many houses were invaded by soldiers who raped girls and women. After it happened in our town, people started leaving. My husband was one year short of reaching retirement from his position with the government. The war started before that year passed. How unlucky! Assad's forces were looking for him to make him join them. We moved many times to escape from their spies, but they kept finding us. We wanted to live in our country peacefully. That was too much to ask from Assad's regime. They followed us everywhere we went. We were terrified. We came here looking for safety from all of that. We have seen enough terrorism in Syria to make us value being here despite the issues associated with living in a camp. At least we are safe. But my husband said many times we should return to Syria. I told him no every time. I said, "We live together, we die together." He wants to return to fight against Assad. He does not accept sitting at home uselessly. But his knee is injured, so if he falls, it will take him some time to get up. I told him, "If you fall in the battlefield, you will not be able to get up and run. So you are walking toward a meaningless death by choice." He dismisses these remarks. He says he would just go alone, die quietly, and rest. He insists that I should stay here with our children. I refuse. I tell him if he dies, our family dies, too.

The problem is that those who return to fight do not know with whom they are fighting. Their goal is to fight against Assad. To die in Syria. To go back. But this is a problem because sometimes they are misled to fight for opposition forces, or for ISIS, without knowing it. Most men returning to fight are very young. Some are kids. Even if they are kids, they will probably be referred to as terrorists for taking up arms in the war. Young men here and in Syria are lost. We are in a mess. They do not know right from wrong. Some rebel groups were good, but then no one knows if they merged with ISIS or other terrorist groups. We became suspicious of everything we heard.

Our major problem in the camp is not electricity or food. Our problem lies with our young men. If only they could leave for a couple hours a day to work inside or outside the camp and then return, that would change their lives and ours. They need to work and to go elsewhere for some time. They are young and full of energy. They cannot just die sitting. If they leave the camp for a while, their moods will improve. They will be able to forget some of their misery because they are busy with something. Because they will be able to do something of value. Instead, they sit around all day, depressed. I tell them, "My dear children, please be patient. For the time being, I want you to appreciate the food we have when you get hungry, the water we drink when you are thirsty, and the place we stay in away from death."

They look at each other and say ironically, "Look at our mother, look what she is saying." I know they are right. But I will try anything to keep them from returning. They say, "Our mother is kidding. She speaks to us as she would to little children, whom she can convince easily."

I hope the war ends and we return. My daughter's husband promised her he would help her go back to school when we return. Pleased, she looked at him and smiled. My sons passed high school here; they were excellent students. But that was it: there is not a college in the camp that they can go to. We need money to send them to college outside the camp. I was told each student needs five hundred to a thousand Jordanian dinars to cover his college tuition and fees. Where can I get this from? Even in Syria, we relied on their father's salary to cover all living expenses. But education is free in Syria up until you finish college. So they are sitting here now, waiting to return to Syria or for the government here to make new laws allowing them to study outside the camp with financial support. We are told the administration is working to help children go to school at the camp and to create scholarships for those who excel and get accepted at a college in neighboring towns.

My husband was a military policeman. His thirty years of service with the government were wasted. If only war had not broken out, he would be receiving salary and benefits now. It is all gone. This is why he is mad. Losing everything he worked for all his life made him very upset. He comes from a poor family, and the army was their only way of working. He started working at the age of seventeen. He was the provider of the house. But now he is not. He lost his income and job. His health deteriorated afterward.

I am the breadwinner in my household. I started working at the beginning of this year with an NGO. I am thankful. My husband tells me, "Do you think it is easy to see my old wife walk forty-five minutes in the heat every day to go to work and another forty-five minutes to return from work while I sit here doing nothing?" We are the same age. A few days ago I went to check on my married daughter. I found her crying. She said she does not have anything to eat. I took her to our caravan and fed her. I gave her tomatoes, potato, and cucumber to take to her caravan. I told her never to cry because of hunger. We have plenty of food. I told her she was wrong to cry over food and that she should come to our caravan to share what we have anytime. Her husband does not work either. He is looking for a job. Meanwhile, I help them get by as much as I can.

I make forty-eight dinars a month. It helps. Some months I work extra hours and I make more money. As you know, we are not in a position to save money. We just want to make ends meet. Each month one of my sons gets to work for a few days in the camp. They look for jobs all the time, but no one is hiring full-time. The owners of the shops here hire their relatives. Everyone comes and complains to me. I raise my hands only to God. I ask for his deliverance. Anything to help my children. I am willing to do anything to keep them safe here. I cannot see them go back to face death in Syria. It was very hard for us to bring these children into the world. We lost three children before them. They died after I gave birth to them.

"Mother, We Will Take You to Heaven Because We Will Be Martyrs"

My sons tell me, "Mother, give us your blessings to go to Syria to die. We will take you to heaven because we will be martyrs." The middle son tells me, "Please, Mother, let me go. I will be a martyr, and I will take you and Dad and all of my aunts and uncles to heaven. Death for our country and people is better than life." I cannot do anything about this. He keeps bringing it up. I tell him, "If you go, I will never forgive you. I will have a heart attack and die." He says I am lying to him to keep him here. I am scared of the day when this will no longer work, and they will just leave. I am scared this day will come soon. When they argue about returning to Syria with their dad, I beg him not to scream at them or upset them. He listens to me. He knows we cannot afford to lose them. He is a broken man.

I have a brother who has been missing for three years. We do not know his whereabouts. Nothing. When he was first arrested by the Assad regime, we asked about him, but we could not find him. After some time passed on his disappearance, we could not ask about him. My entire family is in Damascus. My husband was in the military, so I had to leave right away. I do not regret coming here. It is for the sake of my children. I will live through any difficulty to see them safe.

I call my mother sometimes. She says we should not come back because our town is not safe. She says I should protect my children and stay where I am. They hear her. She tells us stories of shelling and arrests. The soldiers break into people's houses while they are asleep. They take the men. They also take girls and women. Sometimes they let them return to their houses after being arrested. No one knows what happens to them. We hear stories of rape and torture—so many horrifying stories. I did not wait to see for myself, but what I heard was enough to make me take my children and leave right away. Just before the war erupted, my oldest two sons were supposed to join the army, but we decided to leave. We could not stay because the danger was great.

My daughter is beautiful. I worried that the soldiers would rape her. I wish we could return to Syria, that it would be safe and we would no longer want anything other than being home. We would be fine in our country. We can farm our land. But we cannot return now. Several of my sons' friends were killed, I swear to God. They were fighting with the Free Syrian Army, and they were all killed. One of my son's best friends fought for several years against Assad with the Free Syrian Army, and he, too, was killed. We left everything behind us and fled. We did not look back. No mother wants to see her son killed.

The Demands of Six Children
Fatin

I am here to bring my sister to the doctor. Her blood hemoglobin is very low; it is at 9. She is anemic. She is twenty-two and has three children. She lives outside the camp with her husband. She got very sick. So I brought her here so the doctors could check her blood. We are waiting for her blood results. She cannot eat because she feels pain when she eats.

This baby of mine is ten months old. I have another four sons and a daughter. I am here in the camp alone with my children. I am responsible for the children by myself. I am on my own. I go to the stores and buy stuff. I have to provide food and house needs. There are so many with six children. I am tired. I am sick. I faint suddenly. I cry often. I am away from my family and country. My eldest daughter is sixteen years old. She is studying here at the school. Providing for six children in a camp by yourself is hell.

My teenage son is driving me crazy. It is torture. He fights with the neighbors often. It causes me a lot of stress. I try to solve his problems with the neighbors, but most of the time I cannot. I wish we were in Syria. He started smoking here. He goes out with bad guys. He likes a girl, and he wants to get married—can you believe it? I can hardly make ends meet for him; how can I support another family? Plus he is a kid himself. She does not leave her caravan often, thank God. My husband liked to have children, so we had six. I like children, too. Our society does. I took birth control pills for years, but they caused me terrible headaches and leg pains.

Medical care here is not very good. The waiting line at the clinic is long. I cannot blame the doctors or nurses; there are always plenty of sick people. I hope the lines get shorter one day. Some doctors listen and help. You would hope others would care more.

At least life is better now in the camp than when it was first opened. We heard terrifying stories when the bathrooms were public. Now everyone has a private bathroom in their caravan, which is great. There is still not enough drinking water here. We get water once every ten days. I hand wash our clothes. My eldest daughter helps me, but sometimes we run out of water. Sometimes our neighbors give us some of their water. Sometimes we have to wait.

CHAPTER 6

Rising Amid the Pain

The Choice of Love
Lana

The first time Zeina told me she was in a relationship, I asked her not to mention it again. I could not accept the idea of my own daughter dating. It is not socially accepted, and I worried what people would say.

Something happened one day that changed my mind.

One of her friends was getting married, and she came to our house on her wedding day. The girl could not stop crying, and Zeina was comforting her. She said she was in love with someone else, but she could not tell her parents. They would not approve of the man she had chosen. She was getting married to someone she does not care for and could not share any secrets with her own parents.

She broke my heart.

I then thought of Zeina. What if she is ever too scared to share something with me? What if she needed help but could not even ask me? Maybe she would go crying to other mothers instead of to me. That is what her friend did when I was talking to her. I was scared we would push her to marry a man she didn't want and she would be miserable. How would we know if she does not even tell us? I talked to her father at length. We agreed that fearing she might have chosen the wrong guy should not stop us from making her feel safe to share her feelings with us. We know we love her, and we refuse to see her taken advantage of by men who might not be interested in a serious relationship with her. We worried she might be hurt. But we came to the conclusion that we should not be the ones deciding her future. We should not be overprotective. We agreed that she should only marry someone she wants.

Zeina got married before we left Syria.

She married the person she loved. On her wedding night, she came to me with eyes full of tears and held my hands and said, "Mama, thank you. I am the happiest girl on earth. I will never let you down." It was the best thing I have ever heard. I walked her to her husband and told him to take good care of her and to never disrespect her. We had to come to the camp here, but Zeina stayed in Syria with her husband and his family. Her in-laws live in a safe area, and she is living with them.

I miss her, but I am glad I have a good relationship with her. I am glad she did not have to come here with us. She is a sensitive and kind girl, and you have to be strong to survive here.

Perseverance in Adversity
Suad

I am proud of what women do here. I visit them every week. I tell them to remain strong and optimistic. I know we are all sad and are still grieving, but this is okay.

This is our reality. We need to deal with it now.

I tell them to hide their fear from their children because they need them to be strong. I encourage them to hold their tears in front of their children but to cry at night when they sleep if they must. They need to cry, so they should cry, but not in the presence of children. I tell them it is okay to lie to their children, to tell them everything will be all right.

We are in the middle of war. Whatever we decide to do is the right thing to do.

I am trying not to think too much about anything and forget the present moment. I tell women it is okay to worry about their daughters and sons, but they have to keep them close. We need to be strong, even if we feel tired or defeated.

We are strong women. This is our fight.

Our men go to the battlefield and entrust us with the children. If they return, then we are lucky. If they do not, then we will become the fathers and mothers in our families. Our weapons are our hearts. We will go through this and stand together.

Our children will return to Syria and rebuild it. I tell women all the time, young and old, not to lose their children. This is the real war. The regime wants to crush our children. It will not succeed. Our children are the future of Syria, and no matter what happens during these years, they should not pay the price their fathers and mothers had to pay. I tell women not to let the war turn them into angry women. Not to forget that we are mothers, sisters, and daughters. We are the big heart everyone needs and searches for in the darkest of hours.

I tell my fellow women they should look in the eyes of their children when they feel they need someone to talk to, to cry with, or to look up to. They should embrace them and hold them tight to their chest. They should tell them they love them and they will live for them.

We will get through these hard times, and we will be proud of ourselves. We lost our men, and we cannot afford to lose our children. Our men sacrificed their lives for the sake of our children. For the sake of generations to come. We will not let them or ourselves down.

We will be strong, and we will be fine.

Standing Up to Abusive Men
Hibah

I have four daughters and a son. They are all here with me in the camp. My husband works in one of the shops in the market. He is old, and the money he makes is not enough for a big family. My son has not been lucky in finding a job.

My daughter Eftikar reached the age of marriage. A guy who lived in our district asked for her hand. Her father agreed. I did not know the groom's family, so I went and asked around. You know, in Syria we lived in our town and around our relatives. We knew each other very well. But here there are thousands of people. It is not easy to collect information about a potential groom. I asked around and discovered that the guy is not very good. I told my husband, but he said he had already agreed and that the groom's father is a nice man. My husband hoped the groom would change after marriage or after he becomes a father. I was not happy with this arrangement. But I could not stop the marriage from happening. Eftikar agreed to whatever her father wanted. My family is big. Living here affected many of our decisions. The situation is far from ideal. We have two small caravans connected to each other, but this is not spacious enough for a family of this size.

Eftikar got married to that guy. He was not rich. No one is rich here. Those who have some money did not come to the camp. They were able to live in Amman or other towns. We understand the financial situation here. We did not ask much from her husband. Just enough for her to buy some new clothes and necessary stuff for the wedding. Eftikar is beautiful and clever. Her eyes are as green as mint. Her brown hair is long. Her husband is lucky.

I wished for a better husband for my daughter. But I reminded myself that we are not in Syria. We are here. We are in the camp. I remind myself that things are different now. Families had to lower their standards. We are no exception. To find a good groom for one's daughter is something to be thankful for, especially if there are many of them.

Eftikar got married to that guy. He works as a deliveryman. He delivers heavy goods from the market to people's caravans. He is stingy. He does not give her money. She does not visit us as often as she should. I started visiting her, but their caravan is small. She lives with her in-laws. I did not want to cause her more trouble. I stopped visiting and started sending her brother to check on her and invite her to come visit us. After a few months, she got pregnant. I did not know how to feel. I was happy she would be a mother, but I was also worried. They do not make enough money. Having a baby here is costly.

Eftikar does not complain about her husband often. If she complains, he will mistreat her. I kept praying for her and asking God to make him kind to her. To change him, as her father thought. The problem is that whenever he mistreats her, his family ignores it. One day, she was bleeding from her nose. Her mother-in-law and his grandmother were in the caravan. They did not say anything. They did not interfere. He does not fear God, for if he did, he would not have treated her like this. Many children live in the caravan with them, too. One asks her to fry an egg, another to clean, and so on. She is exhausted. Living with them is getting hard now that she is pregnant.

Not all men here are like her husband. There are many other good guys.

Eftikar's friend got married to a wonderful man who loves and respects her. My daughter is unlucky. Her father does not stand up for her. He does not do anything. Eftikar does not like to complain to us because we have enough problems to deal with. She says her husband comes home late every night and throws his body on the bed. She feels he is not normal. She says he is bipolar. But no one listens to her. I told my husband many times about this. He said that we are in a camp now, and our circumstances force us to accept this. He said my daughter should not leave her husband and return to our caravan. Especially now that she is pregnant. He said she should stay with him and work on her marriage with him. I worry my son will one day go fight him. If this happens, the camp police might throw both of them in prison or hurl them back to Syria. We cannot afford these possibilities now. I wish she could return to live with us. I would love to take care of her. But it is hard for her to return now that she is married and will have a baby. I do not know how to help her. But I am not going to stay silent.

I threatened my husband that I would go to the Family Protection Center and report Eftikar's husband. He said, "If you facilitate her divorce, I will leave you." I know these things are interfamily and the camp administration cannot do much about them. But at least they can threaten to throw her husband in prison or hurl him back to Syria if he hits her again. I am planning on going to the center soon. This is the least I can do. My brothers and relatives are not in the camp. Had we been in Syria, I would have handled this situation differently. Had we been in Syria, she would have been married to a better man. Being in the camp means life is already tough. Abusive men exist inside and outside the camp. They are everywhere. As there are good men, so there are bad ones. Everywhere. But this does not mean we have to put up with abuse. I was against this marriage from the beginning. I knew he would not change. Once bad, always bad.

The next time Eftikar visits us, I will convince her to stay here. Her husband is happy she is pregnant with a baby boy. I will not allow him to take her for granted. He needs to know that her family is behind her, that we do not approve of his abuse of our dear daughter. If he wants to see his wife and baby, he will have to change his ways. He will have to behave. I will take matters in hand by reporting her husband and by talking to her seriously when she visits us. I do not fear my husband's threat to leave me if I do something to result in my daughter's divorce. I know he will not leave me. He just says so when he is mad. But even if he does, my daughter's marriage is more important to me than my marriage.

We have come here from different towns and villages, with different traditions and habits. I was in the market a few days ago, and there were more than two thousand young men sitting there, doing nothing. I thought to myself, *These two thousand young men could liberate Syria if they wanted to, instead of sitting here doing nothing. Why are they sitting here doing nothing?* This husband of my daughter, why is he pretending to be strong and tough? If so, why doesn't he go liberate Syria? All these young men are good at is getting married and then divorcing girls.

Ridding Oneself of the Refugee Mentality

Thinking like a refugee hurts everybody, especially little girls. Society labels and targets women more than men. A man divorced his wife and freely went on with his life. He got married again within a few months.

The divorce hardly affected him. The divorced wife did not marry again. She was young and jobless. She became the talk of the district. She was blamed by everybody. She was called immature and impatient. If she complains, she is whiny. If she stays silent, she is weak. As a female refugee, everyone encourages you to put up with life and go on. But why? Have not we lost enough by leaving home and becoming refugees in the desert? Why give up the last remaining beat in our hearts? Why see these little girls give up their lives so men continue to dominate? They are scared of divorce. But divorce is not a new phenomenon. Divorce existed in Syria and will continue to exist here. It is a normal part of life. God mentioned it in his book. It is not the end of the world. This is what we should tell our daughters. They should not feel pressured to accept abuse because they are afraid of divorce.

Men use divorce as a tool to do as they wish. They always did. But what if we teach ourselves and our daughters to face this demon?

Parents here say because we are refugees, we will have more divorces. It just is expected to have such things happen to us and to our daughters. The divorce rate is very high here. We are refugees already: we cannot also be refugee women, divorced and with children. Our problem is in the way we think. But who is the victim? These little girls. What is their guilt? What did they do? Nothing. We are the ones to blame.

My second daughter, Najah, saw what happened to her sister, and now she swears every day that she will not agree to marry anyone. But I do not know if she can say no to her father if a groom comes to ask for her hand. She might be able to escape for a few years, but she cannot do so forever. If you are a single female in the camp, you will get married sooner rather than later. I know some good men here, and I hope one of them will ask for my daughter's hand—but not anytime soon. There is no hurry.

I lived all my life in our town in Syria, and I never had bad days like these in the camp. It is just suffocating to be here. People get mad quickly, and the heat and cold kill any optimism. If the conditions stabilize on the borders, I am taking my children and going back. Whether my husband likes it or not, we will return. This camp might work for some desperate people, including us a few years ago, but not anymore. There must be a place for us somewhere in Syria. We have nothing here, and we have nothing there, but at least if we get there, we will survive. The social pressure here is unbearable. I feel like there are problems no one can solve.

A Thousand Chickens

Say you gather one thousand chickens and put them in one small cage. You tell them to adapt to this life. What do you think happens? Following their natural instincts, they will smash each other and compete for air and water. The ones at the bottom of the cage will struggle to breathe. But there are hundreds of other chickens on top of them, suffocating them. Then some chickens will have chicks, because it is God's will. And those chicks will also compete for space and basic survival needs. As time goes by, it only gets worse. Some chickens are bad, and some are good. But when you mix the good with the bad, you can no longer distinguish them from each other. It is just too much to handle.

Some chickens will slip through the bars of the cage in an attempt to breathe or save their lives. They might not know where exactly they are going, but they have to save themselves from this madness. The cage keeper cannot comprehend the numbers of chickens in the cage and how fast they multiply. He extends the cage. But it feels smaller and smaller. He tries to make the life of the chickens better, but whatever he tries, it is just a cage in the desert.

You see, my daughter, this is my story. I am as old as one can get, but I am not stupid. I am fair, and I am patient. But I am telling you, this camp cannot become a city, as some are calling it. It is okay to stay here for a year or so, but you cannot see yourself living here forever. Tens of thousands will return, if not this year, then next year. Some may like it here because they can live safely and get by without having to pay a penny, but we cannot. For us, life is not about eating and drinking. You cannot just start over at the age of sixty after fleeing the horrors of ISIS and Assad. You cannot simply say we have to adapt and be thankful we are not dead. You cannot fix the world. You cannot put up with shit for the sake of surviving. I survived Assad's regime for decades. I survived war. I can survive the camp. I can survive the desert. I can survive human vileness. But I do not want to. I refuse to.

I am old and will die within ten years from now at most, but what about the young children I have? If we do not return as a family, I will help them return by themselves. Danger? There is no danger. Danger is in accepting being a permanent voiceless refugee here. Had we been in a village in Jordan, I would have adapted to life here because my children would have opportunity.

Independence Is Key
Tibah

I cannot tell you much. Our struggle is similar. My story is not unique. Like everyone else at the camp, I lost dear ones to the war. I saw people bleed and die under the rubble. I saw houses leveled to the ground. I saw enough to make me question a lot of things.

War was a turning point in my life. When war erupted, people started moving from one town to another to protect their lives. I did not choose war. But I chose to stay in Syria. I decided to challenge Assad and his men to the last minute. I lived through shelling and survived the worst days in my life. The force behind this was responsibility. I have been responsible for others as well as myself from an early age. Responsibility made me tough. It made me fearless. When the lives and well-being of others are your responsibility, you have to be strong. You have to stand still and persist. I had no time for questions. I enjoyed rising to the challenge and becoming an independent woman. Hardships train you to have a vision. One hurdle after another, you learn that they are temporary obstacles. Once you overcome them, they no longer scare you.

I brought up my brother since he was a baby. He had a special place in my heart. He loved me as his second mother. He decided to stay in Syria when Assad's forces attacked our town. I decided to stay, too. One day, our house was bombed. My brother died instantly. I saw his dismembered body in front of me. That was it for me. We did not expect the events to escalate this fast. I never thought our house would be bombed. Somehow, we wanted to believe everything would be okay soon. We refused to leave. But when my brother was killed—when his life was instantly taken by Assad—there was no reason for me to stay. There was no reason for me to deny the ugly face of war.

Death hit close to home. War took my brother and my home.

I did not want to leave. My in-laws left the town right after the war started. They asked me to join them. I said, "Never, ever!"

My husband and I lived in a small room in a town controlled by Assad's forces for nine months. Not once did he leave the house. I left once a week to buy bread and groceries. Back in Syria, I worked as a hairstylist for years. With my hard work, I was able to support my family when the town was under siege. That meant a lot to me. We did not ask for help. We helped ourselves.

One day, Assad's forces came to our room to look for men. My husband was hiding behind the stairs. They did not see him. He was with neither the Free Army nor Assad. I wished I could continue living in the Free Army's territory because I loved helping them. I used to wash their clothes and cook for them during the first few years of war. But when my brother died, I had to leave. I did not fear Assad's forces, but the way they entered our room made me reconsider my decision. They are criminals. What do you expect from them? They are not Syrians. I have a disabled daughter. One of the soldiers threw her on the ground like a toy. Did I want to see something similar to this happen to my daughter again? No. Could I have done something about it? Yes. Leave the town and seek refuge somewhere else. For her, I would do anything.

Several of my relatives were demonstrating in Damascus and Daraa against Assad. Assad's forces put my family name on a blacklist. Whenever they found anyone with the same family name, they captured and tortured him. I have another brother. He is thirty. He has never participated in demonstrations. When they learned he was at home, they attacked his home and captured him. It has been years. We still do not know what happened to him.

We learned that Assad's forces were deciding on whether to arrest us or kill us. My husband bribed one of the security men. We escaped in the middle of the night. We gave him all we had and fled to Jordan. We were shocked by how complicated the process of arriving at Jordan is. We learned we needed someone to sponsor us so we can stay in Amman. I lived in Amman for nine months while we waited for our IDs to be issued. We paid a lot of money to get these IDs. But we thought it was worth it. We were safe in Amman. We needed the IDs to work and put our children in schools. We were ready to make a life for ourselves in Amman until war ends in Syria. The IDs were issued. We started feeling some sense of comfort.

One day, we were walking in one of Amman's streets. A government security man stopped us. He asked for our IDs. We showed them to him. To our shock, he said they were fake. He said they were not issued by the government. He said we would have to leave Amman and go to al-Zaatari Camp.

Six Months without Electricity

When we first arrived at the camp, the situation was bad. We lived for six months without electricity. I used to have an automatic washing machine, but here I had to hand wash everything. You see how dirty this place is. You see the sand in our eyes and clothes. Imagine hand washing everything, and for no good reason. It is as dirty after washing as before washing.

Water is a big problem, too. Look at our faces: we have become black. We walk for hours every day. Then you have to buy new shoes. How many shoes can a refugee afford? Walking here is different from walking anywhere else. Look at my daughter's shoes. Look. Is this humane? Look at her feet. I hope life will get better. But I am not sure about that.

Thank God, my husband is a good man. He respects me and gives me all he can in the camp. He made us a private bathroom and bought us a washing machine recently. I did not live the tough life women lived when they first arrived here in 2012 and 2013. I heard the living situation was impossible. But these determined women rose to the challenge and managed with so little. They cooked, cleaned, looked for jobs, supported their families. They listened to their children. They became the only possible home for their children. The only remaining warmth.

Waiting for Something to Happen

I have been here for eight months. I am waiting for something to happen. I am trying to get someone to bail us out so we can leave the camp. But it is very hard. We are always told to adapt and get used to life here. But I refuse to. If only we did not lose the electricity so often. Imagine, the food in the fridge and the clothes in the washing machine. I still have to hand wash everything sometimes because we lose electricity and I cannot use the washer. This takes a week. By the time I am done washing, I have to start over because there is more to wash. I have three children, ages two to thirteen. They go through so many clothes.

I feel safe here. I do not worry a lot about my children being in the camp. We used to hear scary stories about al-Zaatari when we were in Syria. But it is not as bad as people say. I live around people from my town at the camp. They are kind to us. They make us feel at home sometimes. It is just the daily challenges that bother me. Adapting to the weather in the desert is not easy. I have to walk everywhere. There is no transportation. I walk to the markets and carry everything back under the blazing sun. It is so hot here. It is unbearable.

I work for the UN. Thank God. I hope each family has one person working. It is difficult to get by without a job. The camp administration gives everyone in the camp twenty Jordanian dinars a month, but is this enough? Do you just eat? Do you not need to spend on other stuff? Even food, would you say twenty dinars a month is enough, especially when you have children?

My husband could not find a job here, so I am the one who works. I started looking for a job as soon as we arrived. It took me four months to find this job. The women come here to do handicraft work. They also come to talk. It is better to talk than to keep silent. I had a brother who had a very good job when he was in Syria. He has a family, and their life was good. Now he is struggling with depression and other mental issues. He needs to buy diapers for his baby. He cannot always do so. He tried to work, but there is no work here. No one hired him. His wife sells some of their food coupons to get money to pay for other stuff they need. It is not enough. I help them every month. We help each other. His story is the story of the majority of families here. You just do not know what else to do when you are cornered like this. He is the man, and he is responsible for his family. When a man cannot provide the basics to his wife and children, he starts doubting himself. Questioning his self-worth. Wondering what role he plays. This creates tension between people. Parents struggle to keep things quiet. Parents fight over silly things. You just cannot control what triggers you.

My sister-in-law and my brother are a good couple. I saw how their relationship changed under pressure in the camp. They started arguing more and more. Being unable to provide for his family and seeing them struggle affected him. She cries when they fight. She said she wants to return to her family in Syria. But she cannot leave her children here. She, too, is staying until something happens. Everyone is waiting for something to happen. For war to end. For a miracle.

I have another brother. He used to sell water in Syria. He lived a decent life. Now he carries water gallons to people's caravans. But he does not make much. It kills his back. But it is a job, after all. And oh, people fight over water here all the time!

My daughter goes to school every day. One day, I went to her school to check on her. I found the children crying and screaming. I asked the teachers, "Why are they crying?" They said, "We do not know." At least they do some kind of studying, which is better than nothing. I teach my children at home every day. When we arrived, the academic semester had already started here. It took me a couple months to get my children into the school. You see, you do have to fight for your rights. Everywhere. I refuse to sit and wait. You do not get served. You serve yourself, and others in the process.

My relationship with my husband remains good. It is not as good as it used to be, of course. But it is good. He takes pills to help him sleep. We try to avoid fighting. We know we need to do our best. He sees how hard I work for the children, and I see how he is trying his best. It is just hard for men to sit jobless and waste their time doing nothing. It feels like they are going to lose their patience. You may sit idle for a few months. But then it gets old, and you feel like you are dying slowly.

We need more jobs.

One possibility I thought of is letting men leave the camp during the day to work in the nearby towns. This would have a positive impact on our lives. The camp is suffocating. The desert does not have a lot to offer its refugees. It is true that there are more than five thousand shops in the camp. Some people have businesses. Some came with money and opened a family store. But that's just 5,000 of 80,000 to 120,000 people.

Living in a small caravan is like living in a box.

We keep busy with anything. Some women are really old. Some are learning how to read and write. Some did not have jobs in Syria. Here they learned to work, and they do amazing stuff. We always look for an opportunity to work and be useful. It is important to feel productive. To feel useful. That gives life meaning. That makes you want to wake up in the morning.

That gives you hope. It makes waiting possible, and less painful.

A Private Space for Women
Suraa

More than 150,000 of us were living at the camp by 2013. It was chaotic; it was impossible to organize the camp or serve the newly arrived refugees. Every day a thousand or two thousand or more arrived. The camp had no space for these thousands of people. Several Syrian refugees burned their own tents to object to the living conditions, to make the camp administration replace their tents with caravans. But the numbers of refugees were so high. The camp administration promised them caravans when it received more money from international organizations. And as time went by, everything started to get better. Frankly, when we arrived in late 2013 it was not perfect, but it was not like in 2012 or early 2013. Now the camp administration is able to offer better services. Nearly half the refugees have returned to Syria.

Many refugees sold their caravans and tents and left. We used some money we brought with us and sold some of my wedding jewelry to buy a second caravan. This made a great difference in the quality of our life. We chased a family for weeks to get them to sell us their caravan before they left for Syria. They sold it to us for five hundred Jordanian dinars. We have a bigger place. We have a private bathroom, and we have a living room. This is a great thing. This solved a problem that affects people's life in the camp. Space is one of the biggest challenges here. When you get two caravans instead of one, you can live a better life. You can sit in one room and sleep in another. The children can sleep in one room and the parents in the living room. I know big families living in one caravan. This has created problems and tensions for them, especially when people are jobless.

It is true that we are not living here like we lived in Syria. But we were in our country; now we are refugees here. In our first year, I was depressed and mad like everyone else. But I looked around me. I heard the news of horror and death in Syria. I closed my eyes and remembered the scenes of bloodshed and destruction in Syria. I decided to do my best here to live for my children. My husband and I had two choices: either complain all day long and wish to return or do the best we can to settle down and make a life for ourselves here until things change.

Refuge from Death

When you see death with your own eyes and lose family members to the war, the first thing that comes to mind is to seek refuge from death. We came to Jordan to stay alive with our children, and we did. The next thing we thought of was keeping our hearts and minds alive. We show our children that we are strong and that we are luckier than some who were stuck in Syria and lost their lives. We needed to be strong for ourselves as well. We never forgot Syria. We think of it every day. We will return when things change, and life will be better. But this is what we have now. Complaining about life and the camp will not change anything.

We try our best to live within our means. My husband leaves every morning and looks for a job. I tried to work, but I could not find a good job, so I decided to take care of my family while my husband works outside the house. It has been okay so far, and it will only get better, God willing. You know, I once worked in a hair salon here, and I dreamed of buying my own caravan and opening my own salon. Every day women came to the salon to change their mood. To have their hair done. To talk. I liked being there because I was able to take my son and daughter with me, and I did not have to spend long hours outside the house. The hairdresser had bought the caravan with another woman. I worked with them for three months and made some cash. It was very nice to make money. It felt good to help my husband. Then they were not making enough money, so they had to ask me to leave. I started working for free to learn from them, but when I had another baby I stopped going.

I wish I had not sold my jewelry when we first arrived and could buy a caravan now. But I hope my husband's work will help us save some money. Maybe in a few years I can open a salon with another woman. I need to be busy with something other than the housework. I also want my daughter to go to school and get a college degree. Perhaps she can work in one of the schools here. I have a high school degree, which does not get you a job. I know some women who went to college in Syria. They were able to find jobs at the camp. I want my daughter to have this opportunity. I heard they are letting some students study at a university nearby called Al al-Bayt in al-Mafraq. It is a very good university. If my daughter goes there, she will be able to work when we return to Syria.

Oh well, I hope we do not have to stay here for another twenty years. That would be sad.

CONCLUSION

Do Not Be a Bystander

On our last visit to al-Zaatari Camp, we met Asma, a ten-year-old girl. She sat at the threshold of her family's caravan. She wore a colorful scarf and held her brother in her lap. We smiled at her. She smiled back and hid her face behind her brother for a few seconds. Like many refugee children, Asma found herself taking on an adult's responsibility. Her mother praised her for helping her take care of the children. She explained that Asma no longer wanted to play outside like she used to in Syria. The status of camp refugee had robbed Asma of her childhood and of her natural emotional and psychological development. It kidnapped her dreams and threw her into chaos in a way that adults are unable to understand. It disrupted her peace.

Asma's gaze followed us as we started to leave the caravan. We felt that she wanted to say something. We felt that she, too, wanted to leave, to go beyond the camp. We waved a final good-bye to her. She waved back and smiled.

We thought of Asma and the other children long after we left the camp. In a way we did not leave the camp, or perhaps the camp traveled with us. The conversations and interactions, the looks shared and words left unsaid now formed a living, vivid part of our reality. The majority of the Syrian refugee women we spoke to and learned from made the future of their children their most important goal.

113

Children were the centerpiece of our conversations. The women felt a great responsibility to guard them. They felt the need to minimize the gruesome impact of war on them, at any cost.

The words of these women will help the rest of the world understand some of the challenges that Asma and other children face with their families. These stories will help piece together some of the realities of camp life. Children are the glimmer of light that the adults follow. They are the lantern in a dark tunnel, the future their parents could not make for themselves—the selves they could not be, the opportunities they lost, the potential they could not fulfill.

For your children, you flee war. You leave your loved ones behind. You lose your life and home. You abandon your comfort zone. You walk toward the unknown.

But you also wage wars. You walk into danger and endure pain. You face your worst fears. You embrace death.

When the fight is about your children, you see life and death in a different light. When their lives are at stake, you face your demons and push yourself to limits you did not know were survivable. You face your choices: submit as an oppressed citizen, rebel as a fearless soldier, or demonstrate that you are capable of disrupting the course of power. You realize that your children push you to see another side of yourself. They make you fight for yourself—your true self. They help you find your light, however dim it has become.

To protect your children is to protect yourself. To fight for their rights and freedoms is to fight for your own. To pursue a better future for them is to push yourself to find and understand your weaknesses and fears and to choose to listen to your inner self, to refuse to submit to a life that offers less.

Perhaps the time will come when the children of Syria can share the stories their parents could not share. They may take on new challenges and live different realities—be all they can be and not what they once were. In the society their parents hope will emerge once again, they can say what they want and live as they wish. Perhaps they will set themselves free.

To deny the voices of Syrian refugees is to choose fear over the power that knowledge offers. You cannot claim to be free when you deny others their freedom or silence them, deliberately or involuntarily. When you listen to these voices, even as they fight to be heard over the clamor of war, you join the fight yourself. By speaking out, Syrian refugee women extend an invitation to all of us to exercise our freedom to listen. To learn. To become more human.

There is perhaps a glimmer of light for everybody.

Choose to listen. Choose to do something about the refugee crisis. Educate yourself and those around you about the genesis of the refugee crisis and how to better deal with the flux of information from the media. Support refugee businesses in your community. Get to know a refugee family and welcome them. Encourage donations to international NGOs supporting refugee rights at home and abroad. Attend town hall meetings related to discussions about refugees and national refugee policies. Invite a refugee to a conversation. You will be surprised to learn that refugees are people like you and your friends. They sleep and wake up. They watch TV and hold jobs. They cannot be put in one box or two. They like sports and picnics. They gain and lose. They love and do not. They get their hearts broken. They break hearts, too. Simply, they are human beings like me and you. They joke and laugh. They sometimes cry quietly at night when everybody falls asleep. They can be judgmental, like you and me. So get to know them. Get them to know you.

Speak out. Raise your voice. Do not be a bystander. Do not shield yourself from the truth. Do not choose voluntary muteness and blindness. There has never been an easier time in history to gain access to information on any subject, let alone a critical enduring issue like that of the refugee crisis. Do your homework. Know the facts, follow the developments through credible channels, educate others, share your knowledge, and do not ask what refugees can do for you. Ask how you can be of service to those thrown out of their homes and countries and turned into refugees at the doors of a foreign country. We can learn lessons from those who show resilience in the face of tyranny. Humans have sought refuge in religion. In a higher power. In God. He embraced those refugees with a big heart and wide shoulders. The native people knew nothing about the European refugees sailing to the Americas. They could not ask anyone about those foreigners. They could not speak their language or understand their mumblings. They could not make sense of their violence and uncalled-for terrorism. They sailed across the Atlantic, emancipated some and enslaved others in the process, and made themselves a happy home. The Syrian refugees are neither killing nor enslaving anyone to make a life for themselves. Their relatives are still standing up bravely to despots in their home countries while they wake up every day in countries that are not their own, outside the comfort of their homes, creating a dignified life for their children and contributing to the community they are now part of. Hope of returning to Syria is what sustains the majority of them. Like all of us, they need to cling to hope for something or someone to endure. Is this not the meaning of life, after all? Homeland. Mother. Father. Family. Lover. Child. Friends. Dream. Career. Garden. Purpose. Life, as they knew it, made it, and wanted it.

While governments continue shamelessly to shut their borders and ports to stop refugees from "infiltrating the system," you have a different choice to make. Do not close your mind. Do not mute your voice.

WAED ATHAMNEH

is associate professor of Arabic studies at Connecticut College.
She is the author of *Modern Arabic Poetry: Revolution and Conflict*
(University of Notre Dame Press, 2017).

MUHAMMAD MASUD

is assistant professor of Arabic studies at
the University of Massachusetts Boston.

EBRAHIM MOOSA

is the Mirza Family Professor of Islamic Thought
and Muslim Societies at the University of Notre Dame.

CPSIA information can be obtained
at www.ICGtesting.com
Printed in the USA
LVHW022355260721
693705LV00012B/1533

9 780268 201173